I0079573

WRITE STORIES YOUR READERS WON'T FORGET

————————

A WRITER'S TOOLKIT

————————

STANT LITORE

Westmarch Publishing | 2022

MORE FROM STANT LITORE

THE DAKOTARAPTOR RIDERS

Gladiators
Incursion

THE ZOMBIE BIBLE

Death Has Come up into Our Windows
What Our Eyes Have Witnessed
Strangers in the Land
No Lasting Burial
I Will Hold My Death Close
By a Slender Thread (forthcoming)

OTHER TITLES

Ansible: A Thousand Faces
Dante's Heart

The Dark Need (The Dead Man #20)
with Lee Goldberg, William Rabkin

&

Write Characters Your Readers Won't Forget
Write Worlds Your Readers Won't Forget
Write Descriptions Your Readers Won't Forget
Lives of Unforgetting
Lives of Unstoppable Hope
On the Other Side of the Night

WRITE STORIES YOUR READERS WON'T FORGET

_____

STANT LITORE

WESTMARCH PUBLISHING

2022

The characters and events portrayed in this book are fictitious. Any similarity to real persons, living or dead, is coincidental and not intended by the author.

Copyright © 2022 Daniel Fusch.

Cover art © 2022 by Lauren K. Cannon.
Cover design by Brady Stanton.

All rights reserved.

Stant Litore is a pen name for Daniel Fusch.

No part of this book may be reproduced, or stored in a retrieval system, or transmitted in any form or by any means, electronic, mechanical, photocopying, recording, or otherwise, without express written permission of the author.

ISBN 978-1-7362127-4-5

You can reach Stant Litore at:
www.stantlitore.com
www.patreon.com/stantlitore
zombiebible@gmail.com

Contents

PREFACE | ABOUT THE COVER ART

1 | WHY DOES YOUR STORY MATTER?   1

2 | YOUR CHARACTER'S VOICE   22

3 | THE PLAY OF MIND: THINGS TO DO
WHEN YOUR THEME IS COMPLEX   61

4 | THE GRANDMOTHER'S QUILT: GETTING
INTO THE *WORK* OF THEMECRAFT   82

5 | THE SLENDER THREAD: CREATING A
THEMATIC OUTLINE   99

6 | MASTERING BEGINNINGS, MIDDLES,
AND ENDS   138

AFTERWORD | THE RISKS OF UNEXAMINED
QUESTIONS   164

ABOUT THE AUTHOR   173

for all of you,
the tinkers, the wordsmiths,
the storytellers and talespinners, the troubadours,
the novelists and bards and playwrights,
the children on the playground,
the authors: you have such stories to write!—
this book is for you.

Preface | About the Cover Art

On the cover of this book, you are looking at a detail from a painting by artist Lauren K. Cannon that I commissioned for my work in progress, *By a Slender Thread*, a novel in which one woman leads thousands of refugees out of the smoking labyrinth of a burning city, following the slender thread of her faith and hope. I am going to open up that manuscript to you in Chapter 5 of this book, as an example for us to play with. The slender thread is a good metaphor for the topic of this book, because much of what this book is about is discovering, joyfully, how to locate the slender threads of the themes that really matter to your story and develop and intensify them throughout your manuscript, weaving them into something colorful, riveting, and unforgettable. If, like Regina on the cover of this book, you sometimes feel that your story is in flames and you don't know how to get yourself out of the conflagration you've written, I am excited at the thought that in these pages and through the exercises in this book, you may find your own slender thread again, grasp it, and run laughing or crying through the smoke until you are reunited again with the wild heart of your story. Come! Let's run and let's write!

1 | WHY DOES YOUR STORY MATTER?

HAVING WRITTEN TOOLKITS on character and worldbuilding, I now embark on *theme*. Of these three, it's the one we talk about the least; yet it's also the one that can grant to writers the most scope for creativity and the most opportunity for play. And if you are intentional in handling your story's thematic concerns, you will be able to invite a willing reader along on an emotional ride that will tug at their heart and their head, and that will stay with them a long time. We'll be talking about how to do that in this book.

When I was in elementary school, my teacher taught me that theme was a matter of answering *What does this story mean?* As a writer several decades older, I can say that theme is a matter of answering *Why does this story matter?* That is, why does your story matter to each of your characters, and why does it matter to *you*? Why are you writing *this* story? What specific hold does this tale have on your heart? If you can find the most compelling answer to that question—and write that answer into every scene of your book—then you will have a story that may matter to many readers, too. You will have a key ingredient to making a story readers won't ever forget. There are other ingredients, too; a story needs to be exciting in a particular way, full of surprises and suspense (I will cover that later in this series, when I finish *Write Pacing Your Readers Won't Forget*), and whatever internal journey your character is on needs to be grippingly told (see the book *Write Characters Your Readers Won't Forget*). But, besides these things, your story also needs to be thematically rich. It needs to *matter*.

This is not to say that your story needs to fit into what is generally shelved as "literary fiction." That's a misnomer in any case; all fiction is literary (it consists of letters), and stories are thematically rich to varying degrees and for varying readers. The question isn't what genre the story is, or in what mode it is told or for whom, but whether the story has been told with craft and in such a way as to leave a lasting impression (so that the reader will continue thinking about it, reliving scenes in their imagination, remaining affected by wonder or elation or afflicted by unexpected thoughts, and will want to tell others about the book). A beach read can be thematically compelling and can *matter* to the reader who is enjoying it, at least for a little while, if the author has done their work well and written a story that makes the reader not only feel deeply but also feel that what's happening on the page is "true" or "real" to them. Cherise Sinclair's *To Command and Collar* is electric with thematically rich storytelling, even though, as a novel of BDSM erotica, it is not likely to be taught in a course on literary fiction any time soon. Less erotic and recently more mainstream, J.R.R. Tolkien's *The Lord of the Rings* was much derided in academic circles for decades. (Yale University's Harold Bloom, invited to write an introduction to a collection of critical essays on *The Lord of the Rings*, cut the introduction short at barely 150 words, and used most of them to mock one paragraph of Tolkien's prose, offered without context, for failing to live up to Bloom's standards for what modern prose in a modern novel should sound like). Yet generations of readers report weeping, laughing, and connecting with that story; they report that the story *matters*. Some part of this is doubtless an affection for the fictional world that infuses that story with its wonders and remarkable creatures (Peter S. Beagle famously said that, if given the opportunity, he would be off to Middle-earth in a heartbeat), but much of it is due to the book's thematic intensity, something Tolkien was intentional about crafting. It is a book that has a lot to say to a reader who is willing to engage imaginatively in the project. For example, consider the iconic moment in *The Return of the King* when Frodo Baggins has collapsed on the mountainside, so devastated by his burden and what it has cost him that he can no longer remember the taste of water or of wine, nor of strawberries with cream, nor what spring in his homeland, the Shire, smells like. There, as the volcano spews ash into the sky above them, his friend Sam Gamgee declares, "Come on, Mr. Frodo! I can't carry it for you, but I can carry you!" He heaves Frodo onto his shoulders and *carries him up the side of that mountain.*

It's an emotionally and thematically stirring moment! Part of what makes it so effective is the sheer *contrast* between, on the one hand, the apocalyptic setting of an erupting Mt. Doom and of a war for the fate of the world—the clash of geological and titanic forces—and on the other hand, the smallness of the hobbits, these little people who might be caught in the middle yet who choose not to cower but to act, to do what they can, however small, to make the world less grim. Besides a triumphant expression of friendship and love, Sam carrying Frodo up the mountainside is an answer to the question Gandalf asks earlier in the story:

> "Always after a defeat and a respite, the Shadow takes another shape and grows again."
>
> "I wish it need not have happened in my time," said Frodo.
>
> "So do I," said Gandalf, "and so do all who live to see such times. But that is not for them to decide. All we have to decide is what to do with the time that is given us."

That is one of the prevailing themes throughout *The Lord of the Rings*—the need, when the roads of the world grow dark, to decide what we will do with the time we have. To take action to make it better, to preserve life, to be true to our friends and alliances, to protect our home and the homes of others. That thematic question is asked in dozens of ways by dozens of characters over the course of the story, some of whom answer it with hope, some with despair or madness, some with relentless loyalty: *What will we do with the time that is given us?*

That is far from the only thematic thread in the book; there are many. But it's an example of how a story that may seem frivolous upon a cursory look (filled with orcs and tossings of magic rings into giant volcanoes) can *matter*, and deeply, to its readers—in such a way that many readers will never, ever forget that story. Indeed, some will be quoting it all their lives. Some may cosplay (dress up) as characters from it. Some may name their children after characters they met in that story, or their homes after fictional locations they visited in its pages.

It's possible your own ambitions as a storyteller are more modest. But no matter what level of thematic intensity you're aiming for, finding out why, specifically, the story you're writing matters to *you*—and why it matters to your characters, and how these two are connected—can help you take whatever story you've embarked on and make it a voyage that will prove unforgettable. As author James Van Pelt puts it:

> The joy of writing…is in presenting moments that are vital enough to pay attention to. The writer is like a witness to an event who staggers away from the experience and feels a compulsion to tell the story to others so they too can experience what the writer saw.

To this, I would add that thrilling stories turn their readers into such witnesses, too, struck deeply by the experience they have just had and driven to share the tale.

SURFACING THEMATIC QUESTIONS

A plot functions by provoking the reader to ask questions, and ensuring they are driven to do so by hope, curiosity, excitement, or unease (as in the case of horror fiction). *What will happen next? Will Kya succeed? Will she find a friend? Will she escape this peril?* The reader keeps turning pages to find out the answers to these plot questions, which are all simply more specific variations on the essential plot question: *What will happen next?*

Thematic questions function similarly; the reader is invited to ask these questions in the very opening pages of a story (see Chapter 6 for more on this), and the reader is led to expect that the story they're reading will allow them to participate in the adventure of finding answers to those questions. Whether or not definitive answers are actually found depends on the type of story and especially on the type of reader. Unlike the questions that propel the plot, thematic questions don't have to do as much with the 'mechanics' of the story (*What happens next?*) but with its 'matter' (*Why is it happening? What do these events say to me about life, love, or the human condition?*). Not *what will happen*, but *what will it mean?* Thematic questions ask things like:

- Does love conquer all?
- When the stakes are high, is it better to go it alone, or to assemble a team of trusted friends?
- What is the best way to take a stand against injustice? What ways fail?
- In the crisis at the middle of your life, do you find your way by looking forward or by looking back?
- How do you recover the joy of childhood when you feel it's been lost?
- Do you need to let go of the past or keep it with you?

- Which is a more pressing need—liberty or safety?

These are all thematic questions. The plot of your story creates opportunities for these questions to be asked, and for their answers to be proposed and tested. Your characters—through their words and their choices—*perform* these thematic questions in an entertaining way, inviting the reader to consider possible answers.

The last question in the bullet list above—liberty or safety?—comes up in *Mockingjay*, the third book in Suzanne Collins' Hunger Games trilogy. Some readers were incensed that Katniss Everdeen, their revolutionary, settled down quietly with the traumatized Peeta at the end of the story, and not with the fiery Gale, while other readers (myself included) found that ending deeply satisfying. What Gale wanted most was liberation and adventure; what Peeta wanted most was rest and safety. The question was which of those things Katniss wanted most, in the end—and how similar or divergent that was to what the *reader* wanted most. The readers had been tossed a thematic question and they were either happy or unhappy with how the novel dealt with the question, but neither camp of readers is likely ever to forget the book.

That's an important point. Other than the morality of your protagonist (as in the case of an antihero or a villainous character), the most potentially divisive thing in a story may be the narrative's handling of the thematic questions (and expectations) that it raises. The more a book *matters*, the more likely it is that some readers will be upset by it and others enthused by it. This is not a bad thing—just the opposite. This happens because thematic questions matter. When a book is raising them, we're engaged (first in the privacy of our own heads, and later when discussing the book with other readers) in a conversation that is at once larger than the story we're reading and simultaneously local to it. The stakes feel high, and the adventure is no longer 'safe' for the reader, strictly speaking. It is a commonplace that a great book can change a reader's life—by challenging their perspective, or by growing their capacity for empathy, or simply by prompting them to feel something that either they have never felt before or that they have not felt in so long, they'd forgotten it was still possible to feel it. This might be what distinguishes the 'deeper' read from the 'beach read,' if anything can objectively be said to distinguish them: in a good beach read, the reader *is* still invited to feel that the story matters—for a while—that it does affirm or speak something that's 'true' or 'real'—but the stakes are kept low enough for the reader's overall emotional experience to be one of safety and comfort. There's nothing wrong with that. Some thematic questions are not controversial (or hardly ever are, at least, not within one subculture), yet still are worth asking repeatedly, just so that we can hear the answers again—the same way that we tell our child *I love you and I am proud of you* at the end of the day when we put them to bed before singing them a lullaby; they've heard it before, but the answer to the child's question 'do you love me?' is always worth repeating. Comfort is a good and necessary thing.

A lot of fans of the television show *Law and Order* have told me that part of the good feeling they get from watching it is that, no matter how messed up things are in the story, and no matter how violent, sordid, or corrupt the criminal, in the end the detectives will catch the criminal. Each episode implicitly asks the thematic question, *Will justice win out?*—a question that is understandably important to us. There is a relief for the viewer in finding, at the end of each episode, predictably, that justice *does* win out. The bad guys get caught. The havoc they wreak upon their neighbors or their society is contained at last.

That is a comforting consideration of the thematic question; other stories ask the same question—*Will justice win out?*—but offer significantly less comfort as they explore the possible answers. Still other stories seek to refine or challenge the question itself, asking whether justice and law might not be synonymous after all, or whether one person's law and order might inflict another person's injustice. But *Law and Order*'s particular way of asking and addressing its own primary thematic question makes the show unforgettable to its fans and keeps them returning, episode after episode, to enjoy it again.

Whether the thematic questions in your story are high stakes or low stakes, controversial or 'universal,' the techniques for working with them on the page and for inviting the reader into that experience are the same. That's what I'll walk you through in this book—*how* to surface thematic questions and how to make them sing on the page so that the entire story vibrates with thematic intensity and promise. So that at the end of the story, the reader feels that the story mattered.

Exercise 1

Pluck your favorite novel off the shelf (or load it up on your kindle or other e-reader device). Consider the story. Why does *this* story matter to you? Think about what happens in the first scenes. What do those things mean? See if you can identify a thematic question that this particular book dealt with in a compelling way for you. Write that question down. Now take a good look at it, and consider:

- Why does this question matter to the protagonist, in this book you love? How is it connected to their fears? To the deepest desire of their heart? To their oldest wound?

- Why does that question matter to *you*? What do you feel as you read this question you've just written down? How is it connected to your own lived experiences? To your fears and desires? To your own oldest wound?

- Are there other stories you have enjoyed that explore this same thematic question (or a question adjacent to it)? How do those stories explore that theme differently?

- Is this a question your own stories and characters are exploring? Why, or why not?

Exercise 2

Try to imagine how the story in that favorite novel of yours would play out differently if the author had cared about other thematic questions and not this particular one. For example, in *The Hunger Games*, what if Katniss's deepest desire was liberation rather than refuge? How would her choices be different, and what would her story then imply for the reader? What if her deepest desire was to be respected? What if her deepest desire was to be loved? None of these versions of Katniss would be the character we know, and the story would matter to readers in very different ways. Speculate about it.

What if *The Empire Strikes Back* ended not with Luke being maimed and Han Solo captured, but with a conclusive victory for the protagonists? How would the thematic concerns of the film change, if that were the case? What would the film be 'saying' to us, if Darth Vader slunk away in defeat at the end, if the characters we love united and were able to persist and change the outcome of the story?

Note that the point of this exercise isn't to judge which version is better; whatever our private thoughts, we have the original storyteller's judgment on that in any case, and we have the story they chose to tell. The point of this exercise is to consider how character (in the case of *The Hunger Games*) and plot (in the case of *The Empire Strikes Back*), and other things too, can help to shape the way we readers and viewers pick up on what matters in a story. So take your favorite story and, in your imagination, change things about it. Change a character's motives or their emotional wounds. Change critical events. Play the storyteller's game of "What if?" and consider how each imagined version of this story might suggest different themes, or different answers to the original theme. Consider why that happens.

Exercise 3

Now consider your own story—either one you've written or one you're writing now, or one you want to write. Choose three authors you know of who write very differently from you, and who have differing thematic concerns and perspectives. Imagine that each of them writes a book with the same character and premise that you have in your story. How would each of them approach that premise and that character differently? In what specific way would this story matter to each author? In imagining, for example, how Stephen King, Ursula K. LeGuin, and Nnedi Okorafor would each write your story and what would matter to each author, you might spot your own thematic question more clearly, by contrast. Your story and the way you tell it is uniquely your own—because no one else can ask the thematic questions that are most important to you in quite the same ways and for quite the same reasons as you can.

The three science fiction writers Frank Herbert, Harlan Ellison, and Ray Bradbury once gave a talk to a group of students in California, and as part of the talk, they took a plot idea or premise submitted by the audience volunteered, and each of them came up with a story based on that premise, on the spot. The idea was of a doctor who visits people, particularly children, to give them repeated small doses of death so that over time, they develop an immunity to death. Frank Herbert wanted to explore the religious and political implications of death immunity; Ray Bradbury wanted to explore the psychology of a child receiving doses of death, and of the mysterious doctor providing the immunization; and Harlan Ellison wanted to write a murder mystery. Though all three writers were spinning a story based on the same idea, and though all three writers were (ostensibly) working within the same genre (science fiction), all three proposed stories were profoundly different, because the idea mattered differently and for different reasons to each writer. Each version was concerned with different themes. Exercise 3 is in that same spirit.

If you are still struggling to identify or clarify the thematic questions that your story is concerned with, look at the possible implications of your character's struggle—that is, the implications of the conflict in your story, both internal and external. That is what Herbert, Bradbury, and Ellison did with the doctor who immunizes against death; each of them asked, "What are the implications of this idea?" They were considering a science fiction idea, but you can just as easily ask it of a romance—*What are the implications of this kind of relationship?*—or of a sword and sorcery novella—*What does it mean for the characters and for their world if magic works in this particular way, or comes with this particular cost?*—or of a mystery—*What does the choice my detective has to make imply about justice?* When I wrote *Strangers in the Land* in 2009-2012, I just started with a premise—in that case, the hungry dead rising in the Bronze Age Middle East three thousand years ago—and with a story I wanted to respond to—in that case, the tale of Deborah and Jael in the Old Testament. But I didn't know yet what the story *meant* either to Devora (Deborah) or to myself. To find that out, as I started writing scenes for the book, I also started to list things that I knew so far about the character and her world. For example:

- Devora is an aging judge who receives visions of the future and can resolve disputes.
- In the past few generations, her people have migrated into this part of the world, subjugating and enslaving the people who were already here.

- Her people's burial customs are designed to keep the ravenous dead at rest; these customs are a legacy of past violent encounters with the dead while her people wandered in the desert. The indigenous people do not have such customs.
- Devora's mother and family were devoured by the dead. She blames the subjugated people for the zombie plague.

Looking past the potential absurdity of my fictional premise, consider those four bullets, that quick list of what we know so far about Devora and her world. Just based on that list of four items, what issues might come up in this story?

In my own telling of it, one thematic concern was the issue of how we tell the tale of our dead—that is, how we remember our dead and how we choose to remember our history. Another was the nature of justice and how justice might or must be achieved: Is a just society one in which complete order is maintained? Is it one whose magistrates see all, where little is hidden and everything is witnessed? Or is it one in which each person's suffering is voiced and each person's needs are met? Is that what makes a civilization just? My novel, retelling the tale of an ancient judge in an unjust land, needed to explore this. My lawgiver character would have an opinion on the matter— a thematic answer of her own—but it might be the wrong one, and I would need to engineer a plot that would force her to reconsider it.

Now play Ray Bradbury or Harlan Ellison to my Frank Herbert. Consider that central "conceit" or premise of the dead rising during the Bronze Age. If *you* were to tell that story, what would matter to you thematically? For you, is it a tale about:

- Grief and closure?
- The necessity of unstoppable hope, of "hope against hope," hope against all odds?
- The way in which the seed of our destruction is planted by our actions and watered by our refusal to accept responsibility and learn from our mistakes?
- The power of friendship—or sisterhood—or family—to repel a threat or overcome an obstacle?
- How to honor our dead while also burying them and letting them go?
- What the way in which we honor our dead implies about the way we honor our living?
- The danger of ignoring the past (history ignored will rise up to eat you; the past has real-world consequences in the present)?

Et cetera. Any of these themes might be suggested by the original premise as I have laid it out, or might be made possible by it.

Also, note the play of opposites in the bullet list above. If the story is partly 'about' how we deal with our dead, then we might find our thematic concern by looking to the opposite of our dead—our living. Similarly, if our main character is a judge and an administrator of justice, we might find our thematic question if we search for ways in which that character is unjust. *Why are they being unjust here?* is a question that might lead us down a trail that is filled with implications for character development, turbulent with backstory, and excitingly full of thematic questions—because that exploration gets to what is important to that character, what moral compromises they have made and why. That line of inquiry demands that we examine the friction between their words and their actions, between their stated values and their lived values. Death and life, justice and injustice, memory and forgetting, hiding and revealing, selfishness and selflessness—look for opposites where they are at play in your story. Consider whether your story is likely to hold its opposites in tension, or whether it will privilege one over the other, or whether it will reconcile them in some new synthesis.

Here are two more ways to surface the thematic questions that may be swimming, ravenous and silent as sharks, under the waves of your story:

Exercise 4

What does your character value? Identifying what matters to them beyond just the confines of your plot can help you to clarify what is going on with them *inside* your story. Imagine your character completing the following sentences, and fill in the blanks as your protagonist might:

Before I die, I will _____ at least once.

If I _____, I will have failed at life.

The one thing I must tell my offspring is _____.

At my funeral, I want people to _____.

What I desire most in a mate is _____.

The hero I revere most in the stories of my people once did a thing. This is what that hero did: _____.

Now, look over your answers. What kinds of things really *matter* to your character—and how does your story threaten or challenge those things? If your character believes that failing to provide for their children will mean they have failed at life, then is your plot one that threatens their relationship with their children? Are they separated from their children? After losing their job, and do they skip meals so their children can still eat? If loyalty is what matters to them most, how do they respond to betrayal, and how do they respond when presented with a choice to attain something they have always desired, but only at the cost of betraying someone they regard as family? (If you've seen *Arcane*, consider the case of the villain Silco, for an example of how this dynamic could play out in a character's choices over the course of a long story.) What choices are driven by the values you listed above, and what do those choices suggest about what *really* matters to the character—and to you? Maybe the story's thematic concern has to do with either the necessity of self-sacrifice or the limits to it? Maybe the children in the story are adults, and the protagonist is still sacrificing in a way that is no longer healthy? Or maybe they have always been selfish and now have to unlearn that? These are just examples.

When you find out what your character most values, you can then discover opportunities to make the plot more intense (by challenging their values, by placing them in a position where they have to choose between two competing values that both matter to them, or by exerting pressure on the character to force them to fight for their values, even at great cost, making choices they never could have imagined making).

When you find out where your plot is exerting the most intense pressure on your character, you find your theme—because your theme is the answer to the question, *Why does this plot matter?*

Exercise 5

Now do a similar exercise, but with *you* as the protagonist. Fill in the following blanks, answering as *yourself*:

Life is precious because _____.

When I think about my death, I think _____.

The thing I wish more people knew about me is _____.

The thing I wish more people knew about life is _____.

The thing I hope I'm right about is _____.

What I admire most in myself is _____.

What I admire least in myself is _____.

If I were a protagonist in a book, the thing I'd want to learn, the way I'd want to grow, by the end of the story is: _____.

Now look over your answers. Were you honest with yourself? You're the only one here. I suppose *I'm* here, but only as a sort of authorly ghost who can't actually see what you're writing. So take a look at what you wrote. This is the first half of a quick map of what matters to *you*. That map contains clues for what could matter most in the stories you want to tell.

Exercise 6

Here's the second half of your map for what matters most to you. It's common that we go through life with a lot of abstract ideas that we believe are important but that we rarely take the time to define or illustrate. That lack of definition is a luxury that authors should deny themselves, because storytellers are concerned with taking the abstract and invisible and making it concrete and visible. Our stories matter because of intangible things (love, peace, forgiveness, justice, hope, freedom, etc.) but for a brief time, our stories make those things so visible and so tangible that readers might cry over them; we invite our readers to never forget what they've witnessed. So, take a moment—right now—and define your abstracts. Be clear, but remember that you are a storyteller, not a dictionary or a lexicon; talk about what each of these things looks like, how *you* think they actually work, and talk about what these things really feel like when you have them:

Peace is _____.

Love is _____.

Fear is _____.

Justice is _____.

Peace is _____.

Freedom is _____.

Hope is _____.

Strength is _____.

Now add any additional abstracts that are important to you personally and that may prove suggestive of your values. Maybe, for you, *grace* or *faith* is central. Or maybe *community*. Or maybe *brotherhood* or *kinship*. Or maybe something entirely different. Note that you're not looking for character traits (such as cleverness, creativity, fortitude, or steadfastness), which are a little easier to define; what you're looking for instead are abstract concepts that wield influence in our lives, that we strive for or against.

[   ] is _____.

[   ] is _____.

[   ] is _____.

Now, if you just completed Exercises 5 and 6, you have a simple but powerful map. Look at your story, its events and characters. Where does your story suggest, or touch on, or imply, or challenge some of the statement on your thematic map? In other words, what does your story have to say to *you* as a reader—to you as your story's first reader? *There* are your thematic concerns.

Now present those concerns as questions. You may have an answer firmly in mind (or not), but the shape of your story is your character's struggle with the question. Here are more examples of thematic questions:

- Is "peace" actually possible when issues are swept under the rug, or is peace only possible after surfacing and reconciling conflict? (Is peace a matter of *rest and absence of conflict* or is it a matter of *reconciliation*?

- Does true love exist? If it exists, how might it be attained? If it doesn't exist, what exists instead?

- Which matters more—loyalty to those with you, or achieving the dream?

- What is the essential nature of heroism?

- When you lose everything, what keeps you going?

Exercise 7

Write down 1-3 thematic questions that have occurred to you as likely being important in your story. Take those with you to the next chapter.

Do you have a few thematic questions written down for your story? Okay, then it's time to play. Let's go to Chapter 2.

2 | YOUR CHARACTER'S VOICE

VOICE AND THEME ARE DEEPLY CONNECTED. When something matters to us, *how* we say it can be as important as *what* we say about it. That's true for our fictional characters, too—and the drama of how our characters discover, say, and live what really matters to them is part of what makes riveting stories unforgettable.

A theme without a character might be a lecture or a sermon, an act of teaching or preaching; it is *characters* that make the difference between a sermon and a story. Characters do this by taking something we might otherwise monologue, cry out, or question in our own lives and living it for us (and for our readers) on the page. Through the unique voices of our characters, we are able to express thematic questions and answers in ways that we never could using only our own voices.

In the film adaptation of *Cloud Atlas*, a central theme gets reflected, as in a hall of mirrors, from dozens of voices—and gets refracted through antagonists' voices, as well. Sometimes the theme gets stated in a monologue, sometimes during a dialogue, sometimes in a quick quip.

Consider these examples:

> SONMI-451: Our lives are not our own, from womb to tomb we are bound to others. With each crime and every act of kindness, we birth our future.

> ROBERT FROBISHER: I understand now that boundaries between noise and sound are conventions. All boundaries are conventions, waiting to be transcended. One may transcend any convention, if only one can first conceive of doing so.

> HASKELL MOORE: There is a natural order to this world, and those who try to upend it do not fare well. This movement will never survive; if you join them, you and your entire family will be shunned. At best, you will exist a pariah to be spat at and beaten-at worst, to be lynched or crucified. No matter what you do it will never amount to anything more than a single drop in a limitless ocean.
> —ADAM EWING, *in response:* What is an ocean but a multitude of drops?

All three characters—Sonmi-451 the clone revolutionary and former slave, Robert Frobisher the gay musician, and Adam Ewing the budding nineteenth-century abolitionist—are speaking, each in their own idiom, of the deep connectivity between people, of a shared humanity and of how compassion can transcend any boundary or social convention. Each of the protagonists explores this same thematic answer to the events of the story in their own way. The antagonists (the villains), those voices in the story that compete with the voices of the main characters, articulate an opposite or opposing answer. In the example above, Haskell Moore gives us his best antagonist speech, arguing for hierarchy and order, for separation between peoples and classes. Then young Adam Ewing takes the very metaphor Moore hoped would dismay and dissuade him ("a single drop") and turns it inside out. That is one thing that good stories can do: They can take a metaphor (which is a kind of story in miniature) that our culture has handed us or is trying to hand us, a metaphor that is so small-minded or hard-hearted that it would require us readers to make ourselves smaller in order to fit inside it… They take that metaphor and pop it inside out so that it becomes a big enough story for all of us to feel welcome in. Not just a few, but all. It is our voice—each of our unique voices—that makes this possible, because each time we hear a theme or idea expressed by a new, unique voice in a way we haven't heard before, that theme or idea can sound new to us again, as if we are hearing it for the first time. It can take on new layers of meaning, evoke powerful emotions in us, and invite us to a fresh perspective.

So our characters' unique voices matter. It is a character's choices and the unique voice through which the character articulates why their choices matter that makes a story unforgettable. In the Netflix series *Arcane*, the villain Silco has to choose between independence for his nation and the safety of the girl he has taken in as a daughter (albeit in a decidedly unnerving and predatory manner). The choice calls into question the very values he has espoused throughout the story. He articulates those values during a moment of conflict, when a coup against his authority is probable:

> SILCO: You know what bore us through those times? Loyalty. Brothers and sisters back-to-back against whatever the world threw at us.

He reiterates the necessity of loyalty at different points throughout the narrative—when he reminisces about his betrayal by another character, in his words on how to recover from such betrayal, and in his contempt (and murderous retaliation) for those who turn their backs on him in the present. Silco makes it very clear to the story's viewers that *loyalty* is what he believes matters most to him. Then, in his final choice in the narrative, he must put his own loyalty to the test. He has fought all his life for the independence of his community; will he achieve that at the cost of betraying a daughter? When he chooses to give up everything rather than turn her in to the authorities, we feel how much that choice matters to him, and he articulates it in a way uniquely his own, while dying by her hand:

> SILCO: I never would have given you to them. Not for anything. Don't cry. You're perfect.

You know what bore us through those times? he had told his opponent. *Loyalty.* And, in the end, he holds true to that. There are many things about Silco as a person that are decidedly abhorrent or even terrifying—but, as a character, he commands not only our fascination but our respect.

Let's get *your* characters talking about what matters to them.

Exercise 8

Interview your protagonist. You want to lure them into a monologue, if you can. Your first lure may not work; not everyone monologues. Adam Ewing keeps his words brief, after all. So you may need to keep pressing, asking ever sharper questions. Say things that make you angry, that boil your heart, beliefs and values that are too often commonplace in our culture that you don't like, values that don't fit you, values that you think fit barely anyone. False stories—that is, stories that feel false to you, stories you would have to warp yourself to fit inside. Be Haskell Moore, throw those stories in your character's face and see how they react. What makes your protagonist angry? What makes them sad? What do they say, in their own voice, in rebuttal? It can be an exciting thing to push your character to the point where a thematic statement comes blurting out of them. What *would* your protagonist say, if pressed to it? They may never monologue it within the pages of your actual narrative—you, or they, may not go in for monologues. But, knowing what it is that they *would* say, you can help them say it in a thousand subtler ways over the course of their story.

A monologue has a directness to it that can be useful when you're stuck. If you are writing in third person and your character's voice isn't coming through to you clearly, put them in first person for a page—get out of the way for a bit and let them talk. See what they have to say, and how *they* say it. Then return to the third-person narrative, informed by what you observed when reading the monologue your character came up with.

Here's a different way to tease out your character's unique voice and their particular way of expressing the thematic concern:

Exercise 9

For the duration of just a page or two, give your character a child—even if they have none in the actual story. It could be a child of their own DNA, an adopted child, or simply someone young that they care for. Something terrible has happened; perhaps one of the child's dearest friends has died. Perhaps the child has been told that they have cancer. Perhaps something else. Something that we don't ever want children to have to experience. Give your protagonist the task of being there with them in that hour, of finding what to say—or what to do, if there are no things to say. In the face of death and loss, the act of sitting down together and painting something with the child can *be* a thematic statement. What gets painted could be a thematic statement. What does your protagonist wish to communicate in that hour?

These exercises achieve two purposes: They help you surface themes that matter deeply to you (and to your protagonist), and they help you get at that theme in your character's own unique voice, whether that voice is expressed verbally, or in mannerism and gesture, or in actions, or by other means. Capturing that theme, elusive and lovely as a soap bubble, as it is seen and spoken and *done* by your main character is really key. While many people might speak eloquently of the ethical responsibility to the other, no one else will ever say it in exactly the same words or tone or with the same import as Sonmi-451 in *Cloud Atlas*: "Our lives are not our own, from womb to tomb we are bound to others. With each crime and every act of kindness, we birth our future." What she has to say is something that may sound true to us (or to some of us), but *how* she says it is unique to her. And because of that, how the reader feels when she says it is unique to that story. So you want to get at what your theme might sound like in your protagonist's voice. Then, try capturing it in the voices of your other characters. If you have an antagonist in your story, try capturing your theme's reverse or antithesis in that person's voice.

This is one of the most powerful things about storytelling—the ability for a reader to sit in a fictional person's presence for a sustained time and *hear their voice*, discovering what the world is like to them, so that the reader can experience the world—with its life, loss, love, and laughter—differently or anew, as if for the first time. *Voice* might be the most significant tool you have as a storyteller.

How Theme Gets *Earned*

In working with voice, it's useful to define how your character speaks to the reader—either directly (in first person, as a narrator) or indirectly (through their interactions with other characters in the story). Does your character speak formally or informally? Crudely or decorously? Cautiously or assertively? Are they long-winded or brief? Are they more likely to make statements or ask questions? Do they apologize when advancing an opinion—"I'm sorry, but…"—or do they insist on the reader's fraternity or complicity in their opinion—"you know how it is"?

Explore how your character manages their relationships with others (and, by extension, with the reader). If you are working with a first-person narrator, then you can often address this directly. If your character were aware of the reader, would they be likely to address the reader as their friend, their foe, their publicist, their confidant, or their worshipper?

For example, does your character demand the reader's engagement, like Egret in my novelette *The Running of the Tyrannosaurs*:

> Watch me. I stand tall on the red sand and breathe deep. Inside me, the nanites are rapidly at work, increasing my oxygen intake, quickening my metabolism, honing the chemistry of my adrenal glands. I can hear the snorting of the tyrannosaurs, can you? They don't like the chill air. Neither do I, but in a few moments we will all be running, we will all be slick with sweat, we will all be fiercely alive. And you, every one of you, will be screaming my name.

Or does your character offer to mentor or teach the reader, like Harry Dresden in Jim Butcher's novels (*Fool Moon,* in this case):

> Magic comes from the heart, from your feelings, your deepest expressions of desire. That's why black magic is so easy—it comes from lust, from fear and anger, from things that are easy to feed and make grow. The sort I do is harder. It comes from something deeper than that, a truer and purer source—harder to tap, harder to keep, but ultimately more elegant, more powerful. My magic. That was at the heart of me. It was a manifestation of what I believed, what I lived. It came from my desire to see to it that someone

stood between the darkness and the people it would devour. It came from my love of a good steak, from the way I would sometimes cry at a good movie or a moving symphony. From my life. From the hope that I could make things better for someone else, if not always for me.

There's a confessional aspect to Harry Dresden's voice, as well. Egret demands your worship; Harry confides in you and sometimes assumes a mentoring role, dropping little mini-essays into his narration: *This is why we create. This is why we're afraid of the dark. This is what evil is. This is how you do, or don't, treat children.* Et cetera.

A less explicitly authoritative and ostensibly humbler version of this confessional-instructive voice can be found in Genly Ai, in Ursula K. Le Guin's *The Left Hand of Darkness:*

> I'll make my report as if I told a story, for I was taught as a child on my homeworld that Truth is a matter of the imagination. The soundest fact may fail or prevail in the style of its telling: like that singular organic jewel of our seas, which grows brighter as one woman wears it and, worn by another, dulls and goes to dust. Facts are no more solid, coherent, round, and real than pearls are. But both are sensitive.

Or maybe your character approaches the reader like a supplicant, pleading for the reader's attention or for their response:

> Please hear me. We are all in danger, the most terrible danger; we are all going to die terrible deaths. If you can hear me, if anyone can hear me, remember these words.

That's Malala, in my saga *Ansible: A Thousand Faces*. Like Egret, Malala has demands to make of the reader, but her demands are entirely different in tone. Where Egret sees herself as wielding power over her spectators (though, in actual fact, she is their sacrifice, meant for their consumption), Malala's appeal to the reader is a distress call, an SOS transmitted across time. Both Egret and Malala's lines quoted above comprise the opening sentences of their respective narratives. Yet these characters' voices are different—and they presuppose different relationships with the reader and set different expectations about the plot and themes of their stories.

Louis, in the opening lines of Anne Rice's *Interview with the Vampire*, does a bit of pleading, too:

> Don't be afraid. Just start the tape… Believe me, I won't hurt you. I want this opportunity. It's more important to me than you can realize now.

Or maybe, rather than offering to teach the reader, rather than pleading with the reader or making demands of them, maybe instead, your character insults the reader, either brashly, like Frank Herbert's *God Emperor of Dune*—

> How you feel about this—your petty woes and joys, even your agonies and raptures—seldom concern us. My father had this power. I have it stronger. We can peer now and again through the veils of Time.

—or more subtly and without the conscious intent to condescend, like Sir Able in Gene Wolfe's *The Knight*, who simply makes assumptions about the reader's inexperience relative to his experience, as in the following passage, describing Able's climb out of a dragon-infested underworld up through the barrel cone of a volcano, with an injured companion carried on his back:

> I looked up, trying to see where [that cool wind] was coming from and how tough the slope was going to be up above, and I saw stars. I will never forget that, and I can shut my eyes right now and see them again. You do not know what stars are, or how beautiful they can be. But I do.

Or maybe instead, your character *flirts* with the reader:

> I'm the Vampire Lestat. Remember me? The vampire who became a super rock star, the one wrote the autobiography? The one with the blond hair and the gray eyes, and the insatiable desire for visibility and fame? You remember. ... I was off to a good start when we talked last.

That's Anne Rice's Lestat in *Queen of the Damned*, who flirts with everyone. Notice the difference made by that tease *You remember,* in contrast with Egret's imperative *Watch me* and Malala's desperate *Please hear me.* And notice the difference made by that "we" that *includes* the reader, as if in a conspiracy between lovers (*...when we talked last),* in contrast to the distancing "you" wielded by Sir Able or by Leto the God Emperor. So small a thing as the choice of a pronoun, and what relationships that choice implies, can start to shape a protagonist's voice.

Maybe your character isn't commanding, or pleading, or mentoring, or insulting, or flirting with the reader. Maybe your character is *angry.* Ostensibly, they're mad at another fictional character in the story, but also, by implication, they're either angry at the reader (who is experiencing the lives of these characters vicariously as the story proceeds) or else angry on the reader's behalf (so that the character gives voice to the reader's own umbrage or outrage at the events of the story thus far or at the choices other characters have made). Here are two examples. First, Arthur Watts to Cinder Fall in Monty Oum's *RWBY*, during a scene where Dr. Watts is being held over the brink of a skyscraper and Cinder is threatening to drop him to his death; with nothing to lose, Watts lets her have it:

> Oh, of course you are—because that's just what you do. Isn't it? And how has that worked out for you? You stormed into Freya's room thinking you would take on Ironwood's top fighter and war machine. But you couldn't. And that machine became the Winter Maiden! Oh, and let's not forget your deal with Raven Branwen. Get all your enemies in one place so you'd have a shot at revenge. If only *someone* could have warned you against such a miserable idea! Oh wait, *I did.* But you pushed ahead, and you lost it when all you had to do was *your job*! You think you're entitled to everything just because you've suffered, but suffering isn't enough! You can't just be strong, you have to be smart. You can't just be deserving, you have to be *worthy.* But all you have ever been is a *bloody migraine*!

Watts, a villain in the story, is answering one of *RWBY*'s thematic questions in his own words, from his own perspective. The question is: *What do you do when you get hurt—what do you do when you lose?* The protagonist's (and the soundtrack's) answer is: *Keep moving forward; our bodies are weak and breakable, but the spirit is indomitable.* Watts' adjacent but rather different-in-tone version of that is *Get your act together and move forward in a way that shows your worth; take responsibility; victims don't become victors as long as they think of themselves as aggrieved victims.* In the protagonist Ruby Rose's voice, answers to the thematic question are presented in a tone of hope; in Watts' voice, they are presented in a tone of fury. But both are answering the same question and in surprisingly similar ways. Hearing the same themes and ethics that have been expressed by the protagonist of *RWBY* now articulated by the villain as well, the viewers may find themselves cheering for Watts, to their own surprise; the viewers may have wanted someone to call Cinder out and tell her how it is, for quite a while.

Here's another example of a character whose unique expression of a thematic statement becomes most audible in a moment of anger—directed explicitly at his friend, but also implicitly at any viewers who aren't living up to their potential, too. In Matt Damon and Ben Affleck's *Good Will Hunting*, there is a moment when Chuckie expresses that frustration to his friend Will. (I will place a brief content warning here for profanity, in case reading profanity bothers you.) Here is the scene:

> CHUCKIE: Look, you're my best friend, so don't take this the wrong way. In 20 years, if you're still livin' here, comin' over to my house to watch the Patriots games, still workin' construction, I'll fuckin' kill you. That's not a threat, that's a fact. I'll fuckin' kill you.
>
> WILL: What the fuck are you talkin' about?

CHUCKIE: Look, you got somethin' that none of us —

WILL: Oh, come on! Why is it always this, I mean, "I fuckin' owe it to myself to do this or that?" What if I don't want to?

CHUCKIE: No. No, no, no. No, fuck you. You don't owe it to yourself. You owe it to me. 'Cause tomorrow I'm gonna wake up and I'll be 50. And I'll still be doing this shit. And that's all right, that's fine. I mean, you're sittin' on a winning lottery ticket and you're too much of a pussy to cash it in. And that's bullshit. 'Cause I'd do anything to fuckin' have what you got. So would any of these fuckin' guys. It'd be an insult to us if you're still here in 20 years. Hanging around here is a fuckin' waste of your time.

WILL: You don't know that.

CHUCKIE: I don't?

WILL: No. You don't know that.

CHUCKIE: Oh, I don't know that? Let me tell you what I do know. Every day I come by your house and I pick you up. And we go out we have a few drinks and a few laughs, and it's great. You know what the best part of my day is? It's for about 10 seconds from when I pull up to the curb to when I get to your door. Because I think maybe I'll get up there and I'll knock on the door and you won't be there. No goodbye, no see you later, no nothin'. Just left. I don't know much, but I know that.

In this case, the theme might be summarized as *Carpe diem (seize the day); don't hold back from what you are meant to do—or from what you can do—just because you're scared.* Note the power in how these two monologues communicate potential answers to the thematic questions raised by these two stories. That power is driven by voice. Watts and Chuckie each have compelling, unique voices and unique ways of expressing their emotional lives—and of calling other characters to account. No one else sounds exactly like Chuckie, and no one else sounds exactly like Arthur Watts.

If you have the opportunity, I recommend looking up clips of the actual scenes; Ben Affleck's performance as Chuckie in *Good Will Hunting* may be the best of his career, and Christopher Sabat's voice acting as Arthur Watts in *RWBY* Volume 8, Chapter 10, "Ultimatum," is absolutely mesmerizing to listen to. Though, certainly, these monologues work excellently on the written page, too.

Exercise 10

Write a brief monologue for one of your characters, one in which they are speaking in anger. Then read it aloud, performing it just for an audience of one, yourself. Reading your character's voice aloud can further help you capture the rhythm and dynamism of their unique voice. For that matter, it can be a powerful exercise to hand the monologue you've written to someone you know who has a dramatic voice or a good reading voice and ask *them* to perform the monologue for you. What do you notice about your character's voice when you *hear* it spoken aloud?

If a thematic 'answer' were delivered without a story, if it were offered drily and emptily—say, in a self-help book or on a Hallmark card—it might sound like nothing more than a platitude or an axiom. But in the unique voices of unique characters—characters who move us, startle us, anger us, amuse us, arouse us, or delight us by their words and actions—the 'answer' becomes anything but dry or empty. Expressed in their voices, the theme sounds *real*, because someone real is saying it. Someone who feels real, even though they're fictional. We sit up and pay attention, as we might in our own lives to a parent, a lover, a brother or sister.

For example, consider Penny Baxter's words to his son in the final pages of Marjorie Kinnan Rawling's *The Yearling*:

> You've done come back different. You've takened a punishment. You ain't a yearlin' no longer. Jody… I'm goin' to talk to you, man to man. You figgered I went back on you. Now there's a thing ever' man has got to know. Mebbe you know it a'ready. 'Twa'n't only me. 'Twa'n't only your yearlin' deer havin' to be destroyed. Boy, life goes back on you… You've seed how things goes in the world o' men. You've knowed men to be low-down and mean. You've seed ol' Death at his tricks. You've messed around with ol' Starvation. Ever' man wants life to be a fine thing, and a easy. 'Tis fine, boy, powerful fine, but 'tain't easy. Life knocks a man down and he gits up and it knocks him down agin. I've been uneasy all my life… I've wanted life to be easy for you. Easier'n 'twas for me. A man's heart aches, seein' his young uns face the world. Knowin' they got to git their guts tore out, the way his was tore. I wanted to spare you, long as I could. I wanted you to frolic with your yearlin'. I knowed the lonesomeness he eased for you. But ever' man's lonesome. What's he to do then? What's he to do when he gits knocked down? Why, take it for his share and go on.

That feels *real*. It's in a real person's voice, a person we've just spent 500 pages with. That isn't just a platitude. It feels *earned*. Jody and Penny's story has earned it, and I cried the first time I read it. That is also why thematic answers such as this one often arrive near the end of a story, near the end of a character arc; their journey earns the answer—though we will see an example in the next chapter of what it can look like when the thematic answer is stated at the *start* of a tale rather than at its conclusion.

The reason a thematic answer that is offered to us in a Hallmark card or in a self-help pamphlet might fail to move us isn't necessarily because the answer is wrong or because we don't agree. It's because it hasn't been earned. Our truths are fought for. That's why they matter to us. Truths spoken from one character to another, *in their voice*—when those truths have been earned by the story, by their struggle—can matter to us too. How could they not, if we have been living that character's life vicariously over the course of the book?

Thinking about when a particular thematic answer (or partial answer) has been *earned* can also guide you in its placement in the story; answering thematic questions prematurely can run the risk of making the answers appear frivolous or too easy. In Chapter 5, I will invite you to note where, in each section of your story, critical themes get touched on. As you look that over, one key question to ask is, *As of this scene, has this sentiment been earned? If not, does more need to happen or do other things need to be said before this scene, to earn it? Or does this moment need to come later?*

This is not to say that your story *must* provide thematic answers. Your story might suggest a merely tentative answer, or a few. Or there may be *no* answer at the end, just a scene that places the question before our eyes in the most evocative way possible, a question that the reader must now consider anew in the light of the events and plot that they have just weathered with your characters. At the end of *Waiting for Godot,* the two gentlemen are still waiting, because the uncertainty itself—the absence of an answer— is the thematic concern of that play. The end of Stephen King's novel *The Stand* also leaves its thematic question in the reader's hands, unanswered:

> "Frannie," he said, and turned her around so he could look into her eyes.
>
> "What, Stuart?"
>
> "Do you think … do you think people ever learn anything?"
>
> She opened her mouth to speak, hesitated, fell silent. The kerosene lamp flickered. Her eyes seemed very blue.
>
> "I don't know," she said at last. She seemed unpleased with her answer; she struggled to say something more; to illuminate her first response; and could only say it again:
>
> *I don't know.*

With that final line, *The Stand* doesn't just leave the question unanswered but also emphasizes its probable unanswerability. Will humanity ultimately destroy itself, or will humanity learn not to? *I don't know.* The reader is left holding hope in one hand and unease or fear in the other—fitting for a long novel about extinction and rebirth that vacillates between the emotional registers of epic fantasy and horror.

In your own story, what is that moment like, when the thematic question is raised for the final time before the last page is turned? If one of your characters or a narrator offers an answer at that point, has that answer been earned? And how is that answer "pitched" to the reader? Does your character speak in sorrow or in anger, in the joy of liberation or in the grim determination to fight the long defeat?

The other way a theme can feel earned when spoken is when it's voiced by your characters in a moment of high-stakes conflict. That is because conflict is about theme; theme is what gets expressed through conflict. When I first started teaching the craft of fiction many years ago, I would tell the writers in my workshop to get very clear on what is at stake, emotionally, for each character in any scene of dialogue or conflict. "If there is nothing at stake," I would tell them, "Then why do we even have this scene? Why would the reader want to read a scene where nothing's at stake?" Sometimes, a writer would ask me, "How do I know what's at stake?" My original answer is still a useful one: Identify what your character most desires and identify what they most fear, and you'll then know what's at stake, because our desires and our fears ride us as raiders ride horses.

But another way to answer that question—a way that is productive for a storyteller—is to identify the theme. There are frequently multiple thematic questions at play in a novel or script, but in a given scene, one may be primary. (And *usually* one is primary for the work as a whole; that helps to give a work of fiction clarity, focus, and relentless momentum.) What is the theme? That is what gets expressed in the conflict; it's what gets argued about in the dialogue. It is tied to the character's most profound desires and fears—those passions that surge and ebb inside them as they make the choices that define their lives.

The theme is what's at stake.

Early in the series *Arcane*, viewers find themselves riveted by the two-part argument between Vander and his adopted daughter Vi, after a failed heist. Take a look. The dialogue is masterful. It develops the characters and prepares the plot by clarifying one of the story's thematic questions and thus what is emotionally at stake for both characters—one of whom has answered that question for himself and one of whom needs to. Here's the first part of the argument, in the middle of the series' first episode:

VANDER: What the hell were you thinking?

VI: That we could handle a real job.

VANDER: A *real job*?

VI: We got our own tip, planned a route, nobody even saw—

VANDER: You blew up a *building*. Did you even stop to think about what could have happened to you? Eh? To them? (*gestures at her friends*)

(*silence*)

VANDER: (*sighs*) Where did you even get this tip?

POWDER: We just heard it at Benzo's shop.

VANDER: From?

POWDER: *(hesitates, then in a small voice)* Little Man.

VANDER: *(growls)*

VI: *(leaping to her feet)* I'm the one who took us there. If you want to be mad, be mad at me, but *you're* the one who always says we have to earn our place in this world.

VANDER: I *also* told you, time and time again, the Northside's off limits. We stay out of Piltover's business.

VI: *Why?* They've got plenty, while we're down here scraping together coins. When did you get so comfortable living in someone else's shadow?

(A pause; the room goes quiet)

VANDER: Everyone out.

(The others exit)

VANDER: Sit down.

VI: I'm fine.

VANDER: Sit. Down.

(Vi sighs and sits; Vander then sits down too, across from her)

VANDER: Those kids look up to you.

VI: Yeah, I know.

VANDER: You know, but you don't know. When people look up to you, you don't get to be selfish. You say run, they run. You say swim, they dive in. You say light a fire, they show up with oil. But whatever happens, it's on *you*.

VI: (*sighs*)

VANDER: Just like it's on me what happens to us down here. We make ourselves a problem for Piltover, and they *will* send the enforcers.

VI: *So?* Why answer to them? These are *our* streets. Someone should remind them of that.

VANDER: You're not hearing me. That path? (*takes hold of Vi's bloodied wrist*) This? It's not gonna solve your problems. Just makes more of them.

As a viewer, I'm riveted. I've been a teenager in trouble, and I've been a dad, too. (Am one to this day). I *feel* these lines. It's excitingly well-crafted dialogue. On the level of *technique*, the writer knows when to pause, when to let one character pontificate while the others brood, and when to keep the dialogue moving fast and quick, like a duel. On the level of *themecraft*, this swift scene reveals what really matters to the characters at this point—and to the story. Vi wants to redress injustices (by roguish or even violent means if necessary), and Vander wants his family and his people safe, and he wants the people around him to take responsibility and anticipate the consequences of their actions. Repeatedly in *Arcane*, characters make choices without thinking ahead, without counting the costs of those choices, and many memorable dialogues in the series offer a tug-of-war between young idealists and older, wiser souls who lived through previous conflicts and who know that when you put your war gauntlets back on and stride out onto a bridge, it had better be for a *really* good reason. (Vander, in the end, only does so to protect his children.)

His argument with Vi is reprised an episode later, on the eve of conflict. In that scene, Vi wants to see their Undercity rebel against the powers that be, while Vander is urging caution and delay. The scene is set on the bridge that both links and separates the two halves of the city, just as the characters in the scene are poised between two courses of action. It's also the very bridge where many of the critical conflicts and character-defining moments in the story have occurred or will occur: Here's the dialogue, brief but striking:

VANDER: You still don't understand.

VI: What I don't understand is how you can work with *them*. We were here. We saw what they did. I grew up knowing I'm less than them, that my place is down there. I want Powder to have more than that, and I'm willing to *fight* for it.

VANDER: So was I. I was angry, just like you. I led us across this bridge, thinking things could change. ...If I hadn't, your parents would still be alive. I know you want to hurt the topsiders for what they've done to us. But who are you willing to lose? Mylo? Claggor? Powder? Nobody wins in war, Vi.

And there we go. There's the thematic question, one of the principal thematic questions of *Arcane's* first season: *Who are you willing to lose?* The question in reverse, of course, is: *How far are you willing to go to find a loved one again?* Losing and finding are opposites, the two sides of this thematic coin. And those two questions will drive the story, questions so potent, powerful, and thematic that under their momentum, the story will rattle and crash along its track, doing violence to its characters and tearing at the viewers' emotions—because these are not *small* questions. There is so much at stake in them: freedom, family, forgiveness, loyalty, love. Those early dialogues between Vander and Vi, and many of the other dialogues in the story, *earn* the theme. The events in the story are as big as the events in a Charles Dickens melodrama, and very similar on the face of it: family members parted for years before being reunited amid conflict; redemption arcs; the question of forgiveness after terrible things have been done. All of that. But it never *feels* like a Charles Dickens melodrama. *Arcane* is entertaining in a very different way from *Dombey and Son* or *David Copperfield.* The events allow the writer to play out questions that have become desperately important to both the characters and the viewers, and because the writers of *Arcane* are masters of both themecraft and scenecraft, they consistently ask themselves, from episode to episode, what opportunities are available to play on those twin themes—*Who are you willing to lose? How far are you willing to go to find one you love?*—and which opportunity, among those available, would be most riveting and unexpected, which opportunity raises the stakes as high as they can possibly go.

The unique voices of your characters earn the theme, and the theme ignites your characters' interactions and choices with passionate intensity. In Chapter 1, I provided tools and ideas for how to identify what themes may already be arising organically in your draft—or what thematic questions, more generally, are of deepest interest to you as a storyteller. Here in Chapter 2, you need tools and ideas for finding your character's unique voice, the voice that speaks the theme and speaks it unforgettably.

FINDING YOUR CHARACTER'S VOICE

Our voices—what we say and how we speak it—are shaped by the lives we've lived and by the friction between the pressures placed on us by our world, our community, or our family on the one hand, and by our choices on the other—that is, by how we've chosen to respond to those pressures. By whether and when and how we have given way or pushed back, and by how keenly we have felt the cost of doing so. It is the same with your fictional characters.

To take the first steps in establishing a unique voice, think about:

1. **What does your character want?** *Why* are they telling and living this story? How is the deepest desire of their heart driving their choices and their speech? In what ways does your character's way of speaking reveal their desire?

2. **What does your character fear?** How does your character's fear leak into or infuse their voice? How does it shape how they understand and speak of their own story?

3. **How would they approach a listener?** If they were to share part of their story, how would they relate to, or treat, the reader or recipient of the story?

4. **What is the one thing the character would not easily admit, in telling their story?** And what would drive them to do so or make them feel safe enough to do so?

5. **What is the one thing the character would reveal and share most quickly?** And in what tone? And for what purpose?

6. **What questions or uncertainties does your character have about their experiences?** How might they verbalize those questions to an interviewer? To a lover? To their grandparent? To their deity?

7. **What is their cadence and pacing?** Do they speak swiftly, at a gallop, or briefly, cautiously? Is the pacing of their speech belligerent or calculated? Excited or withdrawn? Do they say things directly and tersely, or do they falter to get their words out? Why? What does this say about who they are and how they interact with their world and with their community?

8. **What idiosyncrasies are unique to their speech?** What mannerisms or turns of phrase? With what phrase do they habitually deflect

tension (or rush to meet it)? How does their voice change when under stress?

For example, think of Tevye's cautious consideration of alternatives in *Fiddler on the Roof*—"on the other hand…on the other hand"—or how, when pressed to give an opinion or take a position, he authorizes it carefully with a quote: "As the good book says…" No one else sounds quite like Tevye, and the way Tevye communicates speaks volumes about how he negotiates his place in the world and how he navigates conflict. Yang Xiao Long, in *RWBY*, cracks a joke or a pun whenever she's scared. Jonas, in *The Book of the New Sun*, habitually attempts to defuse tension when broaching a difficult or uncomfortable topic by sharing a humorous simile, hoping for a smile: "Still, it's a terrible way to make a living. That's what the thornbush said to the shrike, you know." Or think of Fezzik's rhyming in *The Princess Bride* (consider how it reveals to the reader the childlike joy that is at Fezzik's core, and the playful camaraderie of his relationship with Inigo Montoya) or Yoda's reversed verb-before-subject syntax in *The Empire Strikes Back*, which has the effect of making the listener—even reckless Luke Skywalker—slow down and listen to what he has to say. In *Cloud Atlas*, Mr. Meeks responds to every question with "I know, I know," and only says more when he has an urgent request to make; Dr. Henry Goose makes the audience uneasy by interrupting himself with a frequent, wheezing giggle. Think of Mr. Spock's interjection of the one word, "Fascinating," in response to something unusual or dangerous, or his customary farewell, "Live long and prosper." Outside of fiction, looking to public personalities, think of Joe Biden's stutter, Donald Trump's overuse of superlatives ("huge!"; "all the best words"), Barack Obama's elevated diction and deliberate oratory, or Dr. Phil's sprinkling of backwoods proverbs and idioms into his speech ("that dog won't hunt"; "that dog won't stay on the porch").

Exercise 11

First, create an idiosyncrasy in your character's speech, a unique turn of phrase or mannerism that your character uses when scared or nervous, or perhaps when they're angry, or when they're excited. How does your character use that mannerism to navigate their emotion in a high-stakes scene?

Second, place the character in a scene that has them scared, angry, or excited—in other words, a scene that's thematically significant, where your protagonist's desires and their fears are both implicated. Now explore how your other characters react to the way your protagonist communicates in that moment. Are your other characters charmed? Irritated? Infuriated? Do they see through the character's idiosyncrasy and express compassion, realizing *why* the character habitually communicates in this way?

Your character's idiosyncrasies reveal a lot about how they handle conflict—and will give them away when they're scared. Part of the fun is watching other characters react to their idiosyncrasies. Tevye the dairyman gets called on his misquoting of the good book, to his chagrin; Yang Xiao Long gets called on her use of jokes to conceal her fear.

"It's okay to be scared," a friend tells her. "You don't always have to hide it."

Exercise 12

Imagine that your character exists inside a virtual reality simulation or a video game, and their personality is *coded*. It consists of a series of slider bars that can be slid back and forth along a scale of 0 to 100. Now, play God. How would you slide your character on these scales?

Shy (0) _____ Expressive (100)
Cautious (0) _____ Flirty (100)
Reserved (0) _____ Friendly (100)
Calculated (0) _____ Spontaneous (100)
Defensive (0) _____ Relaxed (100)
Secretive (0) _____ Bubbly (100)
Suspicious (0) _____ Trusting (100)

Come up with some sliders of your own. (Or make it more complex by identifying triangles or squares divided into quadrants.) Try to grab some parameters that you've never thought about before. Maybe you know exactly to what degree your character is a wallflower or a social butterfly, but you've never asked yourself whether they're someone who leaps onto a motorcycle with abandon or performs a careful, meticulous circle check before getting in their car.

Now look at your character's deep desire and their strongest fear. Considering these, would you move the sliders one way or the other? How do their desires and fears affect these characteristics?

As you plot your character's position relative to these characteristics, try to imagine how they would speak on a

50

blind date, in a job interview, when cornered against their front door by a verbally abusive neighbor, or while in an argument with an old friend. What do they *sound* like?

Let's look at a few examples of how a character's fears and desires shape their voice. Anne Rice's Lestat fears being forgotten and invisible (and thus, to his mind, meaningless in a cosmos without any meaning beyond what we make), so there is a flamboyance to both his actions and his voice. This flamboyance serves to express one of the story's thematic questions: *What does it mean to live life fully, flamboyantly, taking no moment of beauty for granted, reveling in the sensory experience of life—to live like an immortal, drinking all that life has to offer?* There's a forceful heat and a revelry to this character. Consider these lines from *Interview with the Vampire*, in which Lestat urges the younger vampire Louis to kill:

> LESTAT: You will be filled, Louis, as you were meant to be, with all the life you can hold; and you will have hunger when that's gone for the same, and the same, and the same. The red in this glass will be just as red; the roses on the wallpaper just as delicately drawn. And you'll see the moon the same way, and the same the flicker of a candle. And with that same sensibility that you cherish you will see death in all its beauty, life as it is only known at the very point of death. Don't you understand, Louis? You alone of all creatures can see death that way with impunity. You ... alone ... under the rising moon ... can strike like the hand of God!

Lestat's craving for life, always more life, is expressed here in wildly expressive and predatory terms, and the pace of his voice is a torrent, seductive and compelling. Louis, on the other hand, craves forgiveness, so rather than approaching the reader forcefully and sinking in his teeth, *he* pleads with the reader:

> LOUIS: Is this what you want? Is this what you wanted to hear?

If Lestat's voice is a howl at the moon, Louis's is often a whisper in the dark. Where Lestat's lines are quick and forceful, using a repetitive rhythm, Louis's sentences are slower and longer. He broods. He contemplates. He mourns:

> LOUIS: The magnificent paintings of the Louvre were not for me intimately connected with the hands that had painted them. They were cut loose and dead like children turned to stone. Like Claudia, severed from her mother, preserved for decades in pearl and hammered gold. Like Madeleine's dolls. And of course, like Claudia and Madeleine and myself, they could all be reduced to ashes.

His cadence is slower than Lestat's. Lestat's voice is all about *Let us burn hot as the stars this night until the night is a scream in our blood*, while Louis's voice is all about: *Please hear and remember, because somehow, somewhere, for someone, these lives lost and my life lost must have meaning.*

Or consider Ursula K. LeGuin's Genly Ai, who wants his report to be understood, wants the world he has visited to be recognized, its people recognized to be just as human as the reader and recipient of his report, and yet also recognized as distinctively different and uniquely themselves. He is passionately concerned with this, both because he is devoting his life to living on their world and facilitating communication between the two, and because he is falling in love and deep friendship with one of their people. To have his report be both *true* to its subject and *understood* by people who have not lived and can scarcely imagine his experience or his lover's—this drives him. And this need to set aside even one's most fundamental assumptions and witness and engage with others not in terms of one's categories and prior understanding but instead as they truly are, this thematic concern shapes everything about Ai's voice. He realizes as he sets pen to paper: *I can't make a report about these people in a way that means anything unless I tell the story.* So Ai opens his tale in this way:

> I'll make my report as if I told a story, for I was taught as a child on my homeworld that Truth is a matter of the imagination.

It's an unusual and lovely opening for a book; Ai starts by declaring his method, because the story's thematic concern is about your method of seeing and understanding the other. For Ai, that self-awareness is the prerequisite for finding what he desires in a connection with the other.

When you find what your character desperately wants (and fears), you find that character's voice. And when you find their voice, you find the theme, in all its reality and richness and nuance.

Now let's play:

Exercise 13

First, try variations on a theme, where the variations are different voices. Each of these voices will speak to the same theme—but each will understand and present that theme differently. Some might make a statement. Others might present a question, perhaps desperate, perhaps eager, or perhaps amused and curious for the reader's answer. You get to decide. Each voice will present the theme through the lens of their own life experiences—their own wounds, fears, and dreams or desires. For each of the following characters, write one paragraph in which the character addresses the reader directly, as they would someone sitting with them at a table, and in each case, have the character speak to the theme *Time heals many things*. For the sake of this skillbuilding exercise, your characters are:

> A grizzled veteran of two wars
> A recently bereaved widow or widower
> A youth flush with the new joy of young love
> A president stepping down from office
> A lighthouse-keeper and hermit, speaking to another person for the first time in twenty years
> A mad scientist contemplating genocide
> A person who has just been thrown into prison
> A parent consoling a child
> A judge concluding a divorce case

Once you have completed them, look at the nine paragraphs you've written. How do they each express the theme differently? What idioms are unique to each, what figures of speech? Which characters speak slowly, which quickly? Have each of them noticed quite different things *about* the theme? Which characters' voices sound really compelling, unique, and riveting to read or to listen to? Consider what makes them so. What really *matters* to each character, and for what reason is this theme of *Time heals many things* specifically important to each of them?

Here is an illustrative example I offered in my book *Write Characters Your Readers Won't Forget.* The following two paragraphs express a painful memory, but each gives the memory to a different character. One character is Brutus Secundus, a guardsman from my novel *What Our Eyes Have Witnessed,* estranged from his family and alone; the other is Julia, a patrician woman whose family has lost its wealth and prestige, and who craves a return to the hilltop villas where high society knows your name and cares who you are. In remembering a scene of having witnessed their father beating a slave to unconsciousness, notice how each character voices the same thematic point—*that we have a responsibility to intervene when we witness injustice or cruelty*—and how each character expresses what appears on the surface to be the same sentiment—regret:

> BRUTUS: I was very young, domina. I would have liked to have stayed my father's hand, though it would have dishonored him, and myself.

> JULIA: I was young. I would have stopped him. You would have stopped him. Anyone would have. I wanted to—you have no *conception* of how much I wanted to! Never mind the dishonor. I would have stopped him—I *would* have!

In this case, the two characters are saying the same thing, on a *literal* level. But, because their deep wounds, fears, and desires are quite different, they actually *mean* quite different things. Because our background, our position in society, our lived experiences, and the pressures we experience—that is, our fears and our wounds—all influence the rhythm and cadence of our voices, these two characters also *sound* quite different. Both Julia and Brutus are concerned with the past—fixated on it, in fact. But Julia's sentences are quick and clipped and over with quickly. Julia speaks of her past in a rush, as though desperate to not *really* think about it. She doesn't want to be judged, even by herself. She leaves no time between her words for contemplation of her choices and would probably like to move past this part of the conversation with alacrity. *I would have stopped him, I would have, because I'm that kind of person.* That's all she needs you to know, and that's all she cares to know. The cadence of Brutus's speech, on the other hand, is much slower. He is mulling over the past, considering and reconsidering it. Julia, refusing to be uncertain of herself, emphasizes words more frequently, putting more bite into them as she insists on her version of the past. Brutus's regret is more wistful. Where Brutus wishes to be forgiven for failing to intervene, Julia simply wishes not to be accountable; she wants to forget it—and she can't. It is their variations in cadence, rhythm, and diction (that is, choice of words) that betray to the reader the stark differences in what the characters *mean*.

Exercise 14

Select one of the paragraphs from Exercise 13, perhaps the one you found most interesting. Now, write several new versions of that paragraph. In one, make the character a very different age. In another, change their gender. In another, change their religion, or change (drastically) the details of whatever occurred in their past, while staying true to the one-line description of them offered above. Or change the weather. Let them be speaking these sentences while sheltering from a hailstorm, or in the midst of a long and devastating drought, or on a day as pleasant as paradise, or on "a dark and stormy night." Whether the difference is the degree of social position and power, or clement versus inclement weather, what you are doing in this exercise is altering the specific *pressures* you're bringing to bear on that character and their voice.

If you find this doesn't spark your creativity right away, do this: In each paragraph, give the character a different *secret*. In each case, they want to keep it secret, but this is the paragraph where that secret comes out, whether by accident or by defiant or reluctant intent. Secrets are powerful fuel for plot. A secret is an incredible pressure. Each time you change what the secret *is*, see how different their voice becomes. See whether they express the theme and understand it differently than before. See if they present it to the reader differently—belligerently, where they were hesitant before, hopeful where they were grim, furious where before they were gentle.

Finally, as you work to identify and shape your character's unique and habitual voice, consider the power of scenes in which their voice shifts:

Exercise 15

Choose a character from your story. Now imagine a time when much is at stake, yet your character *is struck completely silent*, so moved by some emotion that they cannot speak. Write that scene. Explore *why* they're silent. Perhaps they want to speak, but they are too hurt. Or perhaps they are holding back so as not to damage a relationship with their words. Why is your character silent? If they are normally a talkative or expressive person, what did it take to render them briefly incapable of speech? What would speech or silence at that moment cost them?

Now, think of one time when much is at stake and your character *can't stop talking.* They want to; they just can't. Write that scene. Explore why they can't stop. If they are normally a quiet person, what would it take to get them to a point where words came pouring out like a flood?

Now, get your character drunk. How does their voice change when they are inebriated? What gets revealed about them to you, the author, as you write that scene?

When we talk about *voice*, pauses and silences can sometimes speak louder than words. And by placing a character in a scene where their preferred way to communicate is suddenly inadequate to their needs, you can learn a lot about who they are, what's really at stake for them, and how *they* understand and react to the themes that are so important to you, their author. Not only that, but in doing an exercise like Exercise 15, you might come up with some great material or some ideas for how a similar moment could play out in your actual story. Scenes when a character who has spoken and acted in a particular way are suddenly driven (whether by great emotion, pain, alcohol, duress, or some extreme circumstance) to speak and act in another—particularly when they then make choices that reverberate for the rest of the story, altering relationships, altering the course of a quest or the course of their lives—those scenes are unforgettable.

I could share other examples. You could have a character who is an aged man, like the bishop at the beginning of Victor Hugo's *Les Misérables*, who speaks in a slow rhythm, answering questions by telling a brief tale or by sharing an anecdote, and deflecting hostility with a self-assured "Just so" before proceeding to reaffirm what he intends to do. The fun for an author in that case is to find the moment when the old bishop loses his temper, when he speaks forcefully at last, with unanticipated heat. You could have a character whose voice is brisk, who always speaks with military efficiency and quick precision, who states his views forcefully but in few words, like Aral Vorkosigan in Lois McMaster Bujold's *Barrayar*, who replies to his father's threat to cast him from the family home with the one-liner, "My home is not a place, sir, my home is people," and who responds to an antagonist's insistence that something cannot be done with the line, "One step at a time, I can walk around the world. Watch me." The fun for an author in that case is to find the moment when Aral speaks in an unaccustomed monologue, the moment when he is so stricken with guilt or some other passion that he is unable to find the military briskness and the quick quip to end the conversation—the moment when his speech becomes reflective, haunted.

Remember the example we began this book with, from J.R.R. Tolkien's *The Lord of the Rings*, of Sam Gamgee carrying his friend Frodo Baggins up the side of an active volcano? Sam is driven to that moment by an extremity of suffering and a deep love, and by witnessing his friend in terrible pain and fear. He is driven not to act "out of character," as the saying goes, but in a way that reveals something deep in his character that hadn't been fully expressed before. That moment, when a shy gardener who likes home and potatoes turns fierce and furious and lifts his friend's body onto his own shoulders, is a moment that readers never forget.

Discover how your characters typically speak and express themselves, and then exert pressure on them and *push* them until *so much is at stake*, until the thematic concerns of the story and the themes of the life they're living are so urgent and immediate that your characters suddenly find themselves speaking and expressing their emotions and convictions in a quite different way—in a way that neither the characters nor the reader realized they could, in a way that makes the reader want to stand and cheer, or that makes the reader want to cry. Write scenes like that.

3 | THE PLAY OF MIND: THINGS TO DO WHEN YOUR THEME IS COMPLEX

SO NOW YOU HAVE A THEME. And you have characters living and speaking that theme inside the formidable pressure-cooker of your story. Now let's talk briefly about *structure*, before we get into the close-up work of crafting thematic intensity over the course of a manuscript (in Chapters 4-6).

Sometimes themes are simple, and an author handles them in a way that is lovely, entertaining, and moving, without being intricate. George Orwell's *Animal Farm* has just one note to play—a satirical one—and Orwell plays it well, building the intensity of that note each time he sounds it over the course of the story. The theme of a Disney princess film can be simple—for example, the theme of the redemptive and transformative power of love in *Beauty and the Beast*—but simple can be powerful. If your inclination and your objective is to deliver a simple thematic answer and to do so powerfully and in an entertaining way, be my guest (pun intended). I love good stories that do that. And whether your handling of your story's thematic concerns is structurally simple or intricate, your story can be thematically and emotionally intense. The techniques I'll share in Chapters 4 and 5 will apply regardless of which course you choose as a storyteller.

Sometimes, though, an author wants to address difficult or multifaceted themes with complexity and through a variety of characters and voices. For the duration of this chapter, let's talk about structuring a theme when you aren't telling a tale that presents the reader throughout with just a single answer to the thematic question. To that end, I'll share a couple of brief frameworks for how you can approach that project in an intentional way—the most common of which is the *play of mind*.

DUELING VIEWPOINTS

Do you remember the examples from *Cloud Atlas* at the beginning of Chapter 2? *Cloud Atlas* (both the book and the film) is an intriguing case because that story *does* offer a singular answer to its thematic question. The question could be expressed in terms similar to these: *Is our society to always be defined by predacity, where 'the weak are meat and the strong do eat,' or is there a way for us to exist that is not defined by hierarchies of predators and prey?* As we saw in Chapter 2, Sonmi-451, Robert Frobisher, and Adam Ewing (as well as many other characters) all discover, articulate, and live much the same answer to that question, but they express it in their distinct idioms. The film builds to a thematic crescendo in which the various stories all reinforce that message, providing it with emphasis and profundity. A single answer to the thematic question is being played in many variations, like a musical composition containing variations on a melody (like the '*Cloud Atlas* sextet' that gives the story its title). This is done in recognition both that the thematic statement must be expressed differently by different characters, with different nuance, in different contexts and in different conflicts—*and* that, like a melody, that theme gains power and resonance through repetition with variation. That is perhaps the easiest way to think about how a thematic question can recur throughout a narrative, accelerating the plot's momentum and increasing the story's emotional stakes each time that theme appears in the story: One answer, spoken and illustrated in different ways, or explored in greater depth, over the course of the tale.

Despite the ultimate simplicity of the theme, however, *Cloud Atlas* is structurally complex, and its strategy of having multiple characters offer answers to the thematic question at multiple points in the story can prove equally useful when your intent isn't to play *one* particular answer (to beat one particular drum) and have it gain resonance at each successive beat, but instead to play with multiple possible *different* answers. What I mean by this is that it's possible (and can be exciting) to set varying answers in conflict with each other, whether the outcome at the end of the tale is that these alternatives finally get eliminated and reduced to *one* viable answer, or whether the tale permits the protagonist and the reader to test the possible answers before finally leaving the question in the reader's hands, to answer by themselves. In that case, the reader has now journeyed through the story and learned to look at that thematic question from multiple angles, they might be more informed or better equipped when seeking their own answer to the story's thematic concern.

My name for this technique is borrowed from scholar Joel B. Altman, who wrote about this method of dealing with thematic questions in *The Tudor Play of Mind*. That book offers a study of how the structure of Elizabethan plays (including the plays of Shakespeare) evolved out of England's education system, where schools taught rhetoric by inviting students to engage in debates in which each would monologue their position. The schools gradually added more dramatic aspects to these performances, until playwrights like John Lyly framed entire debates within dramatic performances of Greek myths. Different characters (performed by different students) would each adopt different stances on a question, and their competing answers would collide over the course of the story. Altman calls the play of mind "the dramatization of a question" and suggests that the plays of Shakespeare and his contemporaries "are essentially questions and are not statements at all":

> The plays functioned as media of intellectual and emotional exploration for minds that were accustomed to examine the many sides of a given theme, to entertain opposing ideals, and by so exercising the understanding, to move toward some fuller apprehension of truth that could be discerned only through the total action of the drama. Thus the *experience* of the play was the thing... Such an experience was, in some measure, set apart from that of ordinary life, so as to provide a leisured *otium* wherein the auditor was

freed to discover or to recall—and then to contemplate—
ideas and feelings not always accessible or expressible in the
life of a hierarchical Christian society.

In other words, the plays of Shakespeare's time—and the
experience of going *to* a play, away from what Shakespeare
called "this workaday world"—permitted listeners to
consider complex themes in a safe and entertaining
environment, and to practice considering those issues from
all sides. In the same way that Pablo Picasso hoped to see
and show a human face more totally by examining it from
every side at once (in cubist painting), some early English
theatrical dramas were written and performed in such a
way as to invite listeners (and later, readers) to look at the
issues that matter to a community from many sides over
the course of a couple of hours.

In *Hamlet*, this play of mind reaches a new level, where
multiple possibilities are entertained and advocated for
over the course of the play by the main character himself;
sometimes, multiple positions are argued within the same
soliloquy, or even the same line. "To be, or not to be?"
Modern readers sometimes dismiss Hamlet (the character)
as chronically indecisive, but in context, Hamlet is in a
situation where he must interpret both what has happened
and what his obligations are based on competing
testimonies and a scarcity of reliable facts, and the play
dramatizes his wrestling with the questions of justice, the
debts we owe to our dead, the role of providence (if any)
in our lives, the best responses to suffering, and even
whether humanity is, or is not, fundamentally good and
noble.

Hamlet was written over four hundred years ago. So what does the technique of the *play of mind* have to offer us today? I would suggest that many works of fiction written in the Western tradition after Shakespeare still employ the rhetorical technique of the play of mind to at least a limited degree. And this technique—of tossing rivaling answers to a question at the reader, in the voices of different characters—can be very productive for today's writers, too. MFA workshops sometimes talk about how certain characters operate as "foils" for the protagonist in a story (offering contrasts that allow the main character's position or choices to shine more clearly).

If, for example, a character (or the reader) is trying to walk a middle road between relying on the head and relying on the heart, there might be two characters in the story that represent the extremes—one who relies too much on the head and not enough on the heart, and one who relies too much on the heart and not enough on the head, as in Jane Austen's *Sense and Sensibility*, where the thematic question is implied by the title (sense *or* sensibility?) and the answer is that it takes a blend of the two (sense *and* sensibility). The use of "foils" is a highly concentrated and familiar form of the play of mind; in this case, the rivaling positions are exemplified by just two characters, but with increasing degrees of nuance and complexity as the story proceeds.

Debates draw our attention and get us fired up, entertained, and engaged—for better or for worse. That is true in a fictional narrative no less than in politics or religion. The debate may be overt or it may be quite subtle, as multiple characters display their moments of wisdom and folly for the reader's consideration. Sometimes, a story revolves around a debate or a contrast in values between a protagonist and an antagonist; in the musical adaptation of Victor Hugo's *Les Misérables*, one of the thematic questions is *Can people change?* and the answers to a second question *To achieve justice, how much order do you need and how much mercy?* are predicated on the answer to the first; Jean Valjean and Javert have opposing answers to that first question—*Can people change?*—and they debate each other several times in musical numbers over the course of the drama.

Speaking of musicals, *Fiddler on the Roof* provides delightful and varied examples of the play of mind. Not only do you have varied characters (a rabbi, a communist activist, a butcher, a butcher's wife in a dream sequence, etc.) expressing different positions on the question of *Does tradition keep us standing, or do traditions need to change with the times?* but you also have the protagonist, Tevye himself, holding debates *with himself*, like a dairyman Hamlet, with only the audience and his God there to listen. Consider this moment, when his tradition requires him to reject the secret marriage of his daughter to a Gentile, even as his love requires him to accept it:

> TEVYE: Accept them? How can I accept them? Can I deny everything I believe in? On the other hand, how can I deny my own daughter? On the other hand, how can I turn my back on my faith, my people? If I try to bend that far I'll break. On the other hand— There is no other hand! No. No. No!

At the end of these lines, Tevye shuts down the play of mind, distraught, but the writers do not—because that scene is not Tevye's final word on the matter.

The play of mind—where different characters mirror each other in performing variations on the thematic question and exemplifying or speaking different possible answers—can be an exciting way to engage the reader more deeply in the story. And if you're aware that you're doing it, that this is the direction in which your story naturally needs to go, you can play with the play of mind in intentional and fun ways. As you identify what positions various characters are (implicitly) taking, you can:

- Create opportunities for characters to perform dueling monologues or dueling one-liners that express or imply their views.
- Pair different characters in different scenes to get particular sparks between divergent viewpoints—including characters you hadn't thought previously about pairing up in a scene together.
- Write moments, especially late in a story, where a character or narrator is able to compare and contrast the views of their companions, colleagues, or enemies.
- Clarify for yourself what is at stake (what thematic answers are in play and possible, and what costs each of them entails) in the most emotional scenes, those scenes when characters have critical choices to make, choices that define or redefine who they are.

I'll share an example of dueling viewpoints from my own science fiction saga, *Ansible: A Thousand Faces*. One way I invited the reader into the *play of mind* in this case is by crafting competing monologues that each permit a character to address the reader directly. In the story, each character is leaving a testimony in the archives of humanity's last refuge. Each wants to sway you to their way of thinking and feeling about the world, because each believes that their way is critical to humanity's future. The monologues are structurally similar and begin with variations on the same opening sentence (with a crucial difference in which human characteristic is being praised), even though the two characters' voices *sound* very different.

Here's Omar's monologue:

> Terror for her burns cold in my blood but I use the fear, letting it make my body swift, my senses sharp. Fear can be a gift. The imams in the Redoubt do not believe this. They wish to achieve unity among the Last of Humanity and starve the fear-eaters through practicing calm—to trust in Allah as an infant trusts in its mother's warm hands. Rasha agrees with them, but none of them understand. Calm will not help us survive. It is *fear* we need. We must grow hard and strong; to do this, we must burn with fear like torches in the night.

> You know this is right. You feel it, each time you gaze out those windows at what awaits us. At what is creeping ever closer, year by year. You feel it in the thunder of blood in your ears, in the wild beat of your heart: your fear keeps you alive.

> Is it any wonder that the ifrits' weapon is fear, that fear is their fuel? The most powerful force in the universe is fear. Fear can transform a herd of wildebeest into stampede, into the oncoming tide, an unstoppable mass of muscle

and bone. Fear can bind together the families and tribes of a million tents into a force that can break continents. Fear can kindle fires and douse them. Fear sets our hands to paper, to keep life-giving knowledge from being eaten by time. Fear builds libraries. Fear makes the heart beat stronger, makes the blood pulse faster, makes limbs swift and hearing sharp. Fear has concentrated all humanity from their scattered cities and dying colonies into this one pyramid, to stand in a protective circle with our backs to the last fire, gazing out at the last nightfall.

You who will one day hear this record of my life, *be* afraid. When this Redoubt cracks at last, hide deep in the earth. Or run far and fast. Your fear is a precious thing—it is what the ifrits desire to eat—it is what they wish to devour. Do not let them. Keep your fear for yourselves. Keep it. Tend it. A day is coming when you will need it.

And here is Rasha's monologue, appearing one chapter later:

The woman presses her fingertips to Sahira's palm, and they touch minds, gently. I can feel it, and see it in Sahira's eyes: the love she has for this woman of a younger era, and for all human beings. Seeing that, my own heart fills with love the way my lungs fill with air. Love is the most powerful force in the universe. Love warms us in the dark. Love makes us kind. Love makes us brave. Love makes us endure through pain and fear until we reach the far side of suffering where all is clear and bright as an ocean of air. Love is gentle as a dove and fierce as a roaring lion. For love—love of those she's lost and those she yet may not, for love of me—Sahira has traveled across the void of time and across the void of space, standing between us and the dark like a bright and blazing flame in a woman's shape. For love, she faces the dawn and she faces the dusk and she faces every midnight. With her love, she has gathered the last of humanity to one hearth, warm as the inside of the earth, warm as her own heart, and yet still she flickers in and out across the dark to defend us.

If all our people loved as she does, nothing could burn us out of the universe. Love like *that*, and God himself would desire to live among us forever, in human form.

So which of them is right—Omar or Rasha? Which is "the most powerful force in the universe" and the preserver of humanity—fear, or love? Which must guide our characters?

It is a thematic question that only the reader can answer. The reader must be the judge of it. The reader must engage in the play of mind, dancing on stage with each of these characters in turn, back and forth throughout the story. That story, of course, won't allow this question to be *played* out on a merely intellectual or philosophical plane; each of the characters will be driven by their fear or their love, will make high-stakes choices that may send the world crashing down about their heads—or save it. In fact, both will have a large part in saving their world, even though neither will be the chief heroine of the story. They are both disciples of Sahira, who is not the viewpoint character; each of them chooses to enact Sahira's vision for the defense of humanity differently.

Dueling monologues are an overt way to handle the eruption of thematic concerns into the drama of your story. You may desire a more organic approach. For example, what does the play of mind look like in *dialogue*, when there is more give and take, more back and forth, and potentially also more direct hostility between characters?

If the luxury afforded you by monologue is *space* (to expound on an idea, all at once, in one great rush of words), the luxury afforded you by dialogue is *time* (to develop a theme in hints and snatches, in flirtations and shy half steps, over the course of many scenes). For example, consider the repartee between the rogue angel Aziraphale and the rogue demon Crowley across multiple episodes of Neil Gaiman and Terry Pratchett's *Good Omens*:

> CROWLEY: It'd be funny if we both got it wrong, eh? If I did the good thing and you did the bad one.
>
> AZIRAPHALE: No! It wouldn't be funny at all.

In another scene:

> AZIRAPHALE: You can't leave, Crowley. There isn't anywhere to go.
>
> CROWLEY: It's a big universe. Even if this all ends up in a puddle of burning goo, we can go off together.
>
> AZIRAPHALE: Go off together?! Listen to yourself.
>
> CROWLEY: How long have we been friends? Six thousand years!
>
> AZIRAPHALE: Friends? We're not friends. We are an angel

and a demon. We have nothing whatsoever in common. I
don't even like you.

CROWLEY: You do.

In another scene:

CROWLEY: You can stay at my place, if you like.

AZIRAPHALE: I don't think my side would like that.

CROWLEY: You don't have a side anymore. Neither of us
do. We're on our own side.

What thematic questions are being wrestled with in scene
after scene of witty dialogue between these two
temporarily corporeal beings? Perhaps *When is it necessary to
rebel against authority?* and *How do you know when you're on the
right side, or if either side is right?* and *Can love transcend any
allegiance, any boundary?*

As playful and full of laughter as *Good Omens* is, it deals
with serious themes, and these are nontrivial questions. It
can take more than just a monologue (no matter how
emotive or powerful) to answer them, because these are
questions that Aziraphale and Crowley have to answer
together, negotiating and examining their answers over time,
putting them to the *test* of time. It takes two (or more) to
answer the question *Can love transcend all other boundaries?*
and it takes a community (even if, in this case, only a
community of two) to answer the question *How do we know
if there is a right side?* So these questions require dialogue,
and a part of the entertainment and joy of *Good Omens* is

that Aziraphale and Crowley are performing the dialogue *for* us; the work of deliberation is off our shoulders. Except that their dialogue *does* make us think. There are moments when we pause afterward to reflect on what we've seen and heard. *Good Omens* offers a play of mind in a comic (and cosmic) setting.

Alright, enough examples. Let's play:

Exercise 16

Pick a moment in your story—perhaps preceding or following an event where much is at stake for your characters. Take a fresh sheet of paper (or open a new document on your computer) and write, at the top, one of the thematic questions that express why this moment in the story *matters*. Now, write a dialogue between two or three of your characters, where each is building a case. They aren't building a case the way they would in court (unless your characters are, indeed, attorneys), but they *are* defending their perspective. This dialogue is limited to one page because it *needn't* be long; in fact, arguments tend to be the most intense and riveting when they are brief. (Take a look again at the exchanges between Vander and Vi, in the previous chapter.)

Here's the catch: For the duration of that one page, everyone speaks in dueling one-liners. Your goal is to find out (a) in how many succinct, compelling, compressed ways each of your characters can state their answers to the thematic question, (b) how distinctly (from each other) your characters can express their answers (for example, which characters get dramatic when pushed, and which state their views in a quiet or understated fashion), and (c) what kind of sparks fly between these characters in this hypothetical scene where, over the course of just a few moments, all the positions get expressed and exposed.

One thing to remember, too, is that a single character can argue different answers to the thematic question at different points in the story. This happens as your character develops and changes, as they get their heart broken and get their heart remade, and as they live and learn and grow. The play of mind is a very adaptable technique across a wide range of narrative types. And, even if you don't plan to use it to *structure* your story, the play of mind can serve a key role for you in designing the thematic tensions and rivaling perspectives in your narrative, by helping you map them out in your own notes.

Exercise 17

Write down one-sentence answers to one of your thematic questions for each character in your story, including minor and incidental characters and including any antagonists or 'villains.' This list of one-liners or mottoes allows you to plot your characters' positions relative to the thematic tensions in the story. Once you have this, take note of which one-liners seem similar. Are they too similar? Do you need more of a play of mind, more diversity in viewpoints to present the reader with, as your characters struggle with each other and with their world?

Or, do you like that they are similar? Are each of the characters playing similar notes with minor variations that are idiosyncratic to each of them? Is there a cumulative effect of these synchronized viewpoints in the story, like a musical composition building toward a crescendo, ultimately inviting the reader's celebration of the answer to the thematic question that the protagonist will find, live, and exemplify?

Give some deliberate thought to this: Should your characters be of one accord on this thematic question? Should there be discordant notes? Should there be more of a diversity of answers? How might each of these authorial choices lead your story to develop a bit differently?

CALL AND RESPONSE

The *play of mind* is a Western storytelling form; it's Shakespeare's method. There are forms in other storytelling traditions that achieve thematic complexity through other means. One of my favorites is *call and response,* a form prevalent in fiction by African American authors and rooted in West African musical, ceremonial, and oral storytelling traditions. Like play of mind, call and response assumes that the audience will help to create the story's meaning, thus rendering the story not only beautiful but useful for the community. In oral storytelling, call and response relies on the participation and improvisation of the story's audience; the storyteller calls out a portion of the tale, and the audience responds, improvising on the tale and making it their own.

In written literature, each novel or short story is a call to which other writers later respond from the audience. Thus, as a reader, you can follow a particular scene through a series of novels written by different authors, each time the scene is "repeated" in a new book, it responds to and revises (improvises on) the previous versions. Thus all stories are connected, each is part of the shared story of the community, and the story remains fluid as it passes from one voice to another. In novels that engage in call and response, the thematic significance of a scene has to do not only with its contents on the page but with the previous scenes that it is improvising on, and what those previous scenes have meant to their readers.

THE MOSAIC

A third way to go about exploring a thematic concern— distinct from the debate of the *play of mind* or the passing of the story from one voice to the next in *call and response*— is to imagine the story as a *mosaic*.

In my *Ansible: A Thousand Faces*, the time traveler Sahira proposes:

> Time is a mosaic made up of millions of tiny events, though Allah alone can see the picture.

Each of these events, each of these scenes, is part of the story of humanity. On a smaller scale, each event and each encounter in a single life is part of the mosaic that makes up that person. The lifetime of an individual, a community, or a species can be perceived not as a plotline but as a collection of moments that attains thematic significance only when seen all together at the end.

Later in the saga, Rasha—Sahira's lover—who once met a future version of herself who had a thousand eyes, adds:

> To be human is to witness the other, and to be witnessed in return: to see and share silence and laughter and pain alike. To know and be known.

> Is that what my eyes mean? That far-future me who looks out at the universe with so many eyes, all over her body? All the moments of a life, all the moments of the life of humanity, every act of fear and each act of love, make a picture that can only be seen with a thousand eyes, a mosaic that only God or a time traveler can glimpse; there may come a night aboard a vast battleship above the earth when I can catch the briefest glimpse of it too—brief, in my periphery, out of the corner of my eyes. I am awed and terrified to think of it, for when that occurs, how will I bear it? How does *she* bear it, my Sahira? …How does she see what she sees and remain human? How does she see and still love?

> Or does she love so deeply *because* she sees, because she cannot see and *not* love?

> One night, I will know.

One of the several thematic concerns of *Ansible: A Thousand Faces* is radical interconnectivity, imagined as a comprehension of all life as a mosaic or as a medley of distinct melodies; harmony requires seeing the whole without losing sight of the individual pieces of the mosaic.

We are not independent of each other but *inter*dependent. At the end of the book, Rasha realizes:

> By story and song, we hold back the dark. Grandmother and her australopithecines knew this, I think. They used to gather under a great baobab on the edge of the savanna and warble together while the dusk fell. The first human song, entering the world at the fall of night. All their eyes shone with it. They linked hands. They sang. It is really always the same song, across all of time, in infinite variations, but always
>
> *the flutter of hope and the beat of the heart,*
>
> the song I sang softly to my son, as a lullaby, when he was in my womb and later, when I carried him bundled in my arms and I was dusty with walking across Syria, my feet cracked, the skin on the back of my hands cracking, my voice cracking… I sing that song that drums in my breast when I think I stand immersed in silence. Heartbeat and hope, loudest in the dark. The heartbeat song that overtakes my whole body when Sahira is in my arms and I in hers, and we are loving. The song that has been sung and chanted and shouted and whispered in a million languages, in a million bodies, on a million worlds, the first song and the last song, the song that is: *We are here, we are alive; nothing will part us; what need have we of a sun in this dark, for there is this fire in our hearts!*
>
> It took me so many lifetimes of walking across the long night to reach this moment, on this ship, but I have been singing at every step, singing all the way.

At the end of her story, Rasha perceives so many moments placed in the mosaic of time, from the origin of humanity in our hominid ancestors, all the way to the end of the universe. What Rasha wonders in the second passage quoted above, and what she experiences in the third, is: *If we could see each moment in the mosaic, would we be moved to love? Or, loving the other without compromise or condition, would we be granted a glimpse of that mosaic? Do we love because we see, or do we see because we love?*

While your own story will be very different from any that I have written, that idea of the mosaic can prove a potent one for you on the level of technique, if what you desire to do is particularly intricate. If your story isn't intended to thrust an answer upon the reader—if you want to lead them gently, like your character, to a deeper appreciation of the theme—then you could place the moments that address your theme into your book as you would place the fragments that make up a mosaic. Only at the end do we glimpse—for just a moment—the big picture. That requires a complexity and intricacy that can be difficult to achieve but that might prove both entertaining and aesthetically pleasing. The film *Magnolia* is structured in this way, presenting a mosaic of moments, each distinct yet each connected thematically to the others. So is the film *Things You Can Tell Just By Looking at Her*, which shares six distinct yet interconnected tales from the lives of six women. The film is poignant in its thematic intensity, in its exploration of loss, and this is achieved not with a linear plot but by setting six pieces, each lovely but fragmentary, into one picture.

Alternately, perhaps you do have a thematic answer, a specific one, in mind, and you *don't* intend to set up a play of mind, participate in a call and response, or craft a mosaic. Maybe your theme is simple and important and needs to be either driven home forcefully or built up in waves upon waves, until the tidal wave of emotion in the final chapters overwhelms characters and readers alike. Maybe you want to show one answer to the reader a dozen times, each time differently—like facets on the same gem, each glimpse of the gem a bit brighter than the last.

Whichever of these models describes your particular pursuit, whether simple or intricate, Chapters 4 and 5 will give you specific techniques for touching on your theme throughout the story, scene after scene, without becoming repetitive or heavy-handed (unless you intend to be).

4 | THE GRANDMOTHER'S QUILT: GETTING INTO THE *WORK* OF THEMECRAFT

SO YOU HAVE YOUR THEMES; you have your characters commenting on those themes, whether wittily or gravely. You have considered to what degree you're working with a play of mind or some other intricate thematic structure. Now you want to dig into the actual scenes in your story. You want to weave the thematic concerns throughout the story more subtly and in ways that keep you (and the reader) focused as you craft and accelerate the story's tensions and as you work out the themes through plot. How do you *craft* a theme, and, in doing so, craft a more evocative and riveting story?

Two strategies I want to introduce in this chapter are *finding the keyword* and *threading the image*. They'll provide you with the techniques to get you playing with your theme in more intentional ways. Then, in Chapter 5, I'll present a way to outline the development of your theme over the course of a story, to help intensify your character development and your plot. Let's get started.

FINDING THE KEYWORD

A *thematic keyword* or thematic phrase recurs multiple times across a narrative (and is sometimes included in the title of the story). Each time the keyword appears, it takes on new layers of meaning, often migrating from its literal usage toward a more metaphorical usage as the story progresses. The repetition (especially if the thematic keyword is introduced in the title of the book) alerts the reader that they need to take notice.

We saw a good example of this in Chapter 2, with Marjorie Kinnan Rawling's classic, *The Yearling.* On the literal level, the yearling is a deer a year old that the protagonist, Jody, adopts and that he has to put down toward the end of the book. The keyword acquires a more metaphorical application when Jody returns home after running away and tussling with starvation. *You ain't a yearling no more,* his father tells him, before offering a speech about how life "tears out" a man's guts, and how each time that happens, he has to "take it for his share and git up" and go on. *The Yearling* is a coming-of-age story, and the yearling functions as a metaphor for youth and for the innocence and play and joyous recklessness of childhood that must be left largely behind if Jody is to survive as an adult in an unforgiving world.

It's a poignant, if tragic, take on coming of age. Jody, living in impoverished backwoods Florida, literally has to put a bullet in his yearling—and, metaphorically, in his childhood innocence—in order to move forward. If the yearling (and, with it, Jody's youthful recklessness) is permitted to live, Jody and his family will starve; the yearling is eating the crops needed for their survival. The memory of the yearling, and the memories of Jody's childhood, remain precious, but the cutting away of innocence toward the end of the tale is as violent as it is necessary.

Yearling is a thematic keyword. It's the title of the novel, it's the topic, and it's a metaphor, one that gets summoned to mind when the reader sees that word. Its significance is interpreted for us first by Jody (through his joy at what the yearling means to him) and later by the fatherly voice of Penny Baxter, who explains as gently but firmly as he can why the yearling had to be killed.

Titles are a great opportunity to cue the reader in to a keyword that is later going to become a metaphor that will prove thematically significant and central to the story. Anita Diamant's *The Red Tent* and Harper Lee's *To Kill a Mockingbird* come to mind, as does Ralph Ellison's *Invisible Man*, which opens its first page with a thematic statement and an explanation of the title and central metaphor of the book. Take a look (pun intended):

> I am an invisible man. No, I am not a spook like those who haunted Edgar Allan Poe; nor am I one of your Hollywood-movie ectoplasms. I am a man of substance, of flesh and bone, fiber and liquids -- and I might even be said to possess a mind. I am invisible, understand, simply because

people refuse to see me. Like the bodiless heads you see sometimes in circus sideshows, it is as though I have been surrounded by mirrors of hard, distorting glass. When they approach me they see only my surroundings, themselves, or figments of their imagination -- indeed, everything and anything except me. Nor is my invisibility exactly a matter of a bio-chemical accident to my epidermis. That invisibility to which I refer occurs because of a peculiar disposition of the eyes of those with whom I come in contact. A matter of the construction of their inner eyes, those eyes with which they look through their physical eyes upon reality. I am not complaining, nor am I protesting either. It is sometimes advantageous to be unseen, although it is most often rather wearing on the nerves. Then too, you're constantly being bumped against by those of poor vision. Or again, you often doubt if you really exist. You wonder whether you aren't simply a phantom in other people's minds. Say, a figure in a nightmare which the sleeper tries with all his strength to destroy. It's when you feel like this that, out of resentment, you begin to bump people back. And, let me confess, you feel that way most of the time. You ache with the need to convince yourself that you do exist in the real world, that you're a part of all the sound and anguish, and you strike out with your fists, you curse and you swear to make them recognize you... Most of the time (although I do not choose as I once did to deny the violence of my days by ignoring it) I am not so overtly violent. I remember that I am invisible and walk softly so as not to awaken the sleeping ones. Sometimes it is best not to awaken them; there are few things in the world as dangerous as sleepwalkers.

Ellison's narrator interprets the metaphor of the "invisible man" for us on the opening page of the story, not on the final page like the metaphor in *The Yearling*. Why did the author choose to open with the explanation rather than end with it? Note the difference. On the one hand, Rawling's authorial voice—coming to us through Penny Baxter on the last page of the novel—claims to be offering a thematic answer that is universal, a shared experience of all who must grow to adulthood in a world filled with hardship and hunger:

> Ever' man wants life to be a fine thing, and a easy. 'Tis fine, boy, powerful fine, but 'tain't easy. Life knocks a man down and he gits up and it knocks him down agin.

Ellison, on the other hand, is not telling "ever man's" story. The narrator of *Invisible Man* is not everyman; his experience is not universal, but is particular to black men, or to some black men, or even to one black man. He is a person who is marginalized, humiliated, and ultimately rendered invisible by the dominant culture—unless he can tell his story in a way that others can hear it. Penny's "ever man" is inescapably visible and evident, but Ellison's narrator would be unseen if he did not collide with us and force us to look at the pressures under which he lives. Because he must assert his existence, Ellison's narrator defines the keyword and key metaphor of the book on its *first* page, then devotes the following five hundred pages to convincing those of us who have not shared his experience how real it is. Where Rawling's tale can conclude with a thematic statement that the reader will accept largely unquestioned, Ellison anticipates the white reader being resistant to his or reluctant to consider it; he cannot take it for granted that the reader will accept his conclusion if it is left until the final page. So he lays it all out up front and then sets about the work of showing the reluctant reader just why that thematic statement has been earned.

Neither strategy is inherently *better;* each is suited to the particular thematic questions of the book—and to the author's assessment of how ready and willing the reader may be to engage with those thematic questions. As you think about your own story, how 'universal' or 'controversial' do you anticipate your thematic questions will be? When your thematic concerns come up, are some of your readers likely to be "sleepwalkers" like those Ellison mentions, who may not recognize or respect your theme? How and when you present the thematic concern to the reader—how directly or indirectly, how aggressively or gently—can be shaped by what kind of journey you think you can take the reader along on. What preparation do they need, if any, to engage with the central concerns of your book, script, or short story? That's worth asking yourself and thinking about very intentionally.

The choice of keyword may reflect this, as well. Rawling's metaphor of the *yearling* speaks to the presumed universality of her theme (coming of age); every spring, we look around us and see yearlings and blossoming plants and signs of youth. The metaphor is familiar. Ellison's *invisible man* is a less familiar apparition; we don't encounter invisible men in our daily lives, or we are not aware that we do. The metaphor is striking, an anomaly, something that requires immediate explanation, something that— ironically—cannot be taken for granted or overlooked once it is mentioned.

Exercise 18

Look at the thematic concerns you've written down in previous exercises and consider: What metaphor might suggest that thematic concern or its answer? What keyword might suggest that metaphor? Here are two ways to explore this:

1. Write one of your thematic questions on a blank page, and then do an idea storm around it, free associating and writing down any terms, ideas, words, images, or sentences that come to mind as you think about that theme. Don't edit yourself; just splash ink across that page. It's important at this first step to record as many ideas and images as you can. Once you have run out of steam, then you can be selective. At that point, reject the easy, expected options—like "dove" for a theme of peace, for example. Look instead for the unexpected connections that your mind made when you weren't censoring it. Maybe you wrote down "quilt." Why? What do quilts have to do with peace? Does it have to do with the way they are made, taking disparate squares of pattern and sewing them together into one unified thing that is both beautiful and useful? Does it have to do with a particular memory (either for yourself or the character in your story, or possibly for both). Were those afternoons with your grandmother, reading or humming or playing with toys while she quilted, the most peaceful afternoons of your life? The answer can be both, of course. Once you have *quilt* as a keyword for your thematic question about peace, you can pull both of those things into the story—the memory of real peace, and the metaphor for how quilts (and peace) get made. Maybe as a child, peace was easy, because

your grandmother had already done the work necessary to provide it; now that you're an adult, you have to do the quilting—and the peacemaking—yourself. Now just translate that idea into your character's voice.

2. Maybe you already have a draft of your story, or drafts of certain scenes. If this is the case, look through your written material with an anthropologist's eye; you are looking for an image, a metaphor, or a symbol that has already surfaced in your story—something fertile with possibility that you just didn't recognize at the time. Maybe your character's car hit a deer in one scene, and you thought it was a throwaway moment, just there to ramp up your character's stress and the urgency of a scene in which your character desperately needs to be somewhere, perhaps to prevent something awful or to do something that will change the course of their life, and that deer is one more obstacle in the way, one more thing slowing them down, one more opportunity for all those emotions to boil over. So you thought it was a throwaway image. But there are no throwaway images, not really; everything is filled with possibilities and opportunities. You just have to learn to spot them. What could hitting a deer on the road mean to your character, beyond the obvious delay? Is your character in such a hurry that they are smacking into other things, damaging relationships, as they go? Are other things in their life as fragile as that deer? What choice do they make in that moment? If the deer is still breathing, do they try to do anything for it? Do they put it out of its misery? Do they drive around and leave it to suffer and die, crushing down a pang of guilt so they can get where they're going? How is that choice—whichever it is—emblematic of their other choices, and how does

that choice interact with the thematic concerns of your story? (For example, maybe your story has something to do with being in a hurry, or with missing what matters in our haste to get through life. Or maybe your story has to do with colliding with people and rushing on without accepting responsibility for the damage caused in our collision.)

Maybe your image isn't a *deer*. (Deer are probably on my mind because we were just talking about Jody's poor yearling.) The deer is just one example of how a seemingly throwaway image can turn into a key that can unlock the poignancy and thematic significance of your story. That's what we'll talk about next: taking that image, once you have it, and threading it throughout your story.

THREADING THE IMAGE

Keywords are powerful because, once interpreted, they provide a shorthand for an extended metaphor; the keyword of the *yearling* or the *invisible man* is essentially a mnemonic device that helps us recall the metaphor and hold it in mind as we dash through the story. Accordingly, keywords often suggest images (unless the invisible man is literally the absence of an image!) or at least specific sensory experiences. (A melody or a smell could function as a keyword and a metaphor too; though I am using the term *image*, largely from habit, it doesn't necessarily have to be a *visual* thing.) Whatever the case—whichever senses are being relied on—you can start adding layers to that metaphor that allow for a lot of playfulness and precision in how you bring the metaphor repeatedly (but not repetitively) to the reader's mind. Just as we encounter Rawling's idea of a *yearling* different times in different contexts—so that the idea means something different and matters differently each time the reader encounters it—so, too, you can take any image you want and have it recur throughout the book, each time in a different context and with different implications.

Exercise 19

Return to the image you identified in Exercise 18. Now brainstorm 10 opportunities to bring that image up in the story, each time meaning something a little different or mattering in a different way.

For example, in the case of the grandmother's quilt, we might come up with moments like these:

1.   The protagonist remembers sitting and playing by their grandmother as she quilted. It was the most peaceful they have ever felt in their life.

2.   The protagonist realizes (perhaps late in the story) that the sewing together of disparate squares into a unified quilt is like the sewing together of disparate lives into a new family or into a community. It takes work, and patience, and kindness, and an appreciation for the beauty each part of the quilt brings that is unique to that part. The result is something that's both useful and beautiful. "Or perhaps beautiful *because* it's useful," the protagonist wonders, "or useful because it's beautiful."

3. The protagonist has to return to their hometown to bury their grandmother. They find the last quilt their grandmother made, and they hold it close.

4. The protagonist's sister has one of grandmother's quilts and has left it in the basement; mice ate much of it. The protagonist finds out.

5. The protagonist's abusive ex-spouse tore up a quilt during an argument.

6. The protagonist visits a store in town while taking care of their grandmother's effects. There are quilts for sale in the store, but they are inferior to the grandmother's. They don't look like they were made with the same attention and loving care. They look "fake" to the protagonist, like pretend quilts. Suddenly, everything in that store—the shopkeeper's smile, the plastic plant in the pot by the cash register—feels fake. Everything in that town feels fake. A town pretending to be a town, pretending to be a community when it really isn't, when it's never been. Too much abuse and grief just beneath the surface, hidden beneath the surface of a fake quilt. Their grandmother understood; it's why she made such beautiful quilts.

7. At the memorial service, a young man who was born in another country shares his memories of the grandmother's visit to his town during her missionary days. He recalls that she didn't preach much or condescend; she was quiet and kind. He used to go sit by her feet, as a boy, and tell her his troubles. She made him a quilt. (Or perhaps, she taught all the women in his town to quilt, and they made a quilt together that

was large enough to cover the floor of a church sanctuary.) The protagonist tries to talk with the man after the service; they had never met. The protagonist is touched and startled to find that they—and this person from the other side of the world—share a common memory of the grandmother, as though they are two squares in the same quilt, two squares that look completely different and yet fit together when sewed there by the grandmother's kind hands.

8. In an early scene in the book, the protagonist is shivering on a winter night. At last, they get up to go start the heat. Nothing's working. Trembling with cold, they pry open an old chest whose lock has rusted, and they get out a quilt, a quilt heavy with the years and warm with memory.

9. The protagonist's family has been torn apart. They try to reconcile with their sister; it doesn't go well before the funeral, but after, the sister reaches out. Maybe the sister comes by in the middle of the night. Maybe the sister walked to the grandmother's house in the rain. When the protagonist opens the door, their sister's hair is stuck slick to her neck; she doesn't have an umbrella. She is shivering and cold, and lonely. She gets out a plastic supermarket bag that she used to protect the contents from the rain, and unwraps the last few squares of the frayed quilt the sister had left neglected in the basement, with the mice. "I saved these," the sister says, not knowing what else to say. "You should have them." After a moment of watching their sister standing in the rain, the protagonist says, "They belong to both of us. Come inside."

10. In the last scene, the protagonist and their sister start sewing a new quilt. The last squares of the sister's mouse-eaten quilt and a new square of some beautiful pattern the man from another country gave the protagonist form the beginning of it. The protagonist doesn't know whether she can quilt or sew a family into existence—family has been torn from so often, by death, by abuse, by neglect—but the protagonist knows they can try. Unexpectedly, they and their sister find themselves laughing together as they quilt.

That's an example of ten moments where *quilt* could come up in that story, each time revealing a little bit more about the thematic concerns, the characters and their conflicts, and each time mattering (emotionally) to the protagonist and to the reader in a new and different way. And because each time we encounter the metaphor of *quilt* something new gets added to it (just like a new square gets added to a quilt), the recurrences of the metaphor don't feel repetitive. It's repetition with variation.

There could easily be more than ten. I say *ten* moments just for the purpose of this exercise.

The story teaches the reader how to read it, by the repetitions of that metaphor. In Chapters 2 and 3, we looked at the use of monologues to snap the thematic concerns into focus, but in the case of this tale of the *Grandmother's Quilt*, when we get to the final scene, in which the sister and the protagonist sit down together to begin making a new quilt, talking and laughing together as they sew the last of the squares from the sister's frayed quilt into the beginning of a new quilt, no monologue is required. The approach is more subtle, but effective—the very activity of sewing the quilt with a long-estranged sister tells the reader everything they need to know at the end of the story and lets them feel everything they need to feel.

When you know what keyword and metaphor matter for your book, you can thread the image throughout the book in this way. And once you have a complete or partial draft, you can look at the scenes that you have and play—you can try to imagine where a quilt might appear in each scene, or how the mention of a quilt in a particular way might heighten the tension and the drama. (Consider that image of the ex-spouse tearing up a quilt, which then becomes symbolic to the reader of so much abuse the protagonist had to endure. Maybe there are other ways the ex-spouse sought to isolate the protagonist and sever them from their past, or from other relationships, or from other things that mattered to them—and the memory of the tearing of the quilt brings all the feelings from all those memories of hurt and helplessness freshly to mind for the protagonist.)

In Chapter 5, we'll talk about tracking where the key image that serves as a metaphor for your thematic concerns appears throughout the scenes of your story. For now, just practice the threading of that image throughout the book—by identifying those ten instances in which the image might occur, each time with a new layer of emotional impact and meaning. Just like that quilt. Most of all, have *fun* doing that! This can be among the most playful of activities for a writer, because now that we know what the image is and what themes it is suggestive of, we can brainstorm all the different ways we could use that in a story. Even in the case of the quilt, you could brainstorm ten ways to use the quilt in a story that I would never even think of—because you and I are different writers. Once you know what metaphor serves as the primary key for unlocking your theme, you could even keep a journal or a running list where you add ideas as they come to you. You can start watching for that image wherever it appears in your actual life, outside the covers of the book. If *you* see a quilt, in what context do you find it? What do you notice about it? Is it frayed and old? Is it well-loved? Has it just been made? Is it hanging on a wall, or is it on a bed, for use rather than decoration? Does it have warm colors or cool? Who made it? Take down notes. Some of it might be useful later.

Exercise 20

Brainstorm a list of alternate titles for your book that each include the image or keyword you identified in Exercise 18. You don't have to actually *use* any of these titles, though you might find one you really like. Or maybe one will become the title of a chapter in the book. The point of the exercise, though, is to think about what each of those titles suggests about the theme. (Remember *To Kill a Mockingbird?*)

For example, for that book about peace—in which the quilt is a key metaphor—maybe we brainstorm the following possible titles:

Grandmother's Last Quilt
No Quilt Survives Her
The Hole in the Quilt
Town Shaped Like a Quilt
My Sister's Quilt

I've been talking so far about defining *one* metaphor that you can suggest with a keyword and that serves as a primary key for unlocking your theme. But although one metaphor is usually primary, you may have multiple metaphors you're playing with. You may also have multiple thematic concerns. In this case, the trick is to consider how the different metaphors are related, and how you might thread them together in new and surprising ways.

Exercise 21

Repeat Exercise 18 and select a second image, a second metaphor, a second keyword. Then look at the list of moments you jotted down during Exercise 19. In which of those moments could the second metaphor make an appearance? How would it make the scene matter even more, if it did? Come up with five such moments in which *both* metaphors appear and are connected.

For example, besides *quilt*, maybe another metaphor in the story surrounding the grandmother's burial is *rain*. It is raining when the sister runs to the protagonist's door. Is the protagonist surprised that the sister was sheltering a scrap of quilt from the rain, rather than the other way around? Does the protagonist have a memory of the grandmother running laughing down a sidewalk in the rain with a quilt draped over her head to keep her dry? When else has rain appeared in the story? Is rain foreboding, or healing and restorative? Did it rain the night that the protagonist completed their divorce? Did it rain at the funeral?

Now step back and think for a moment about what we're actually *doing* here. This is scenecraft! And it's exciting. We are taking an image, discovering how it's meaningful—in fact, listing out lots of different ways and different circumstances in which it can be meaningful to our characters, either helping them to interpret the conflicts in their lives and, in some cases, helping to precipitate or resolve those conflicts—and then we are taking that image and 'hiding' it in plain sight throughout the narrative, in scene after scene, like a basketful of Easter eggs that we hide in the grass on a spring morning for our children to find. Like delighted children, our readers will recognize the metaphor hiding in each scene because it has the same shape each time (like the oval shape of the egg glimpsed nestled between two tree roots or waiting in a flowerpot on the porch), but each time, it's painted a different color and we encounter it in a new place. While the similarity in shape grants the reader comfort and assurance that we're following the track of the story well, the difference in how we encounter each occurrence of the metaphor grants the reader surprise and delight.

Okay, now let's take it up a notch and outline what we're doing. That can help you make informed and strategic choices about where to put certain of your Easter eggs, whether some need to be smaller or larger, or whether some need to be placed further apart or clustered closer together. And, importantly, when and how quickly to add layers of meaning to your metaphor. Next chapter.

5 | THE SLENDER THREAD: CREATING A THEMATIC OUTLINE

PEOPLE TALK ABOUT OUTLINING PLOT, but as I suggested in *Write Characters Your Readers Won't Forget*, the kind of outline you need most may not be a simple summary or plot synopsis, but rather, a separate tool to identify your best opportunities to sharpen the plot. A traditional plot outline, to my mind, has limited utility. A character arc—mapping four to seven key scenes where the character makes critical choices—has more utility for a writer, because it gives you a tool for refining your character development, examining your pacing (where the story needs to move faster or slower), and spotting where additional experiences and plot events are needed in order to heighten the reader's excitement and prepare them for the next moment at which the character has to make a character-defining choice. That's useful.

A thematic outline is a second useful tool—in this case for helping you realize the thematic and emotional potential of each scene in your story, and for taking opportunities in your story that might otherwise be missed. In Exercise 19, I showed you how to take a metaphor that is central to the thematic concerns of your story and brainstorm opportunities to weave that metaphor into 10 scenes in your story, in ways that bring your story to life and that emphasize the stakes. The thematic outline is a next step—it charts *all* the occurrences of your thematic imagery.

To make one, you simply identify each scene of your book in which the thematic thread of your story appears. When you have that list of thematic moments, you can ask: Is the progression of your story's themes beautiful, exciting, and entertaining? Does that progression build tension and nuance over the course of the story? Does your theme get developed or complicated a little each time it gets brought up? If not, maybe there are thematic moments and cues that can be moved earlier or later in your story. Maybe there are moments that are simply missing. Maybe there are moments that need to be made more subtle—or more overt, as seems fitting for that particular moment in your narrative.

If you aren't certain what your major thematic threads are—or which are most important to you and to your characters—then make a list of thematic questions you *think* may be at play in your story, and do a quick thematic outline for each, and see which of the outlines is compelling to you. Which one(s) excite you, and why? Which bore you, and why? Such an exercise can help you keep focused on what *really* matters to you in your story—and can save you a lot of time.

The brainstorm that we did in Exercise 19 can be useful for planning ahead and mapping out how a thematic concern might surface in different points of your story; a thematic outline is a way to capture how that thematic concern actually *is* surfacing, once you have a manuscript or part of one to look at. Then, by revising your thematic outline, you can develop an exciting plan for revising and intensifying your story.

If you are writing by computer rather than by pen and paper, one way to quickly build a rough draft of your thematic outline is to use a Find/Search function to pull up all the places where your keywords appear in the manuscript. Collect all those in one document, label them by where they appear (e.g., what chapter), and then comment on them. Is this where they *should* appear? Do they appear to occur in a logical order? Are there long gaps between appearances?

To illustrate how this might work, I'll take you through the following four steps.

First, I am going to be a little vulnerable and let you join me as I do this exercise *right now*, on a work of my own. I will share a *very* rough draft of the first half of a thematic outline for a work-in-progress of my own. The novel is called *By a Slender Thread*, and it is a historical fantasy in which a young Syrian woman named Regina leads thousands of refugees out of a burning, zombie-infested ancient Rome in search of a new home. At this stage in writing it, I have quite a bit of manuscript written down in draft, but I need to clarify what is happening thematically in my story and make some strategic choices about how I will handle relationships between the principal characters as I revise, and about how they will each end up where they are at the end of the book.

Second, after sharing this extremely rough draft of a thematic outline, I will offer an analysis (and I invite you to analyze the draft outline, as well), noting what gaps may need to be addressed and what revisions might be called for.

Third, I'll share a revised thematic outline for the first half of the same novel, to illustrate where an author can create more thematic and emotional intensity in the story after having drafted an initial thematic outline.

Finally, after we've worked our way through this example together, I'll share some practical advice for wielding your own thematic outline as a device to help you develop your characters and hone your plot.

So I am inviting you into my workshop to observe and participate in this part of my process, and to see the kind of brainstorming and craft that the process of developing and revising a thematic outline makes possible. Let's dive in.

1. SAMPLE ROUGH OUTLINE
(*BY A SLENDER THREAD*)

Exercise 22

Below, I offer a work in progress—a thematic outline for one of the novels I am working on, *By a Slender Thread*. This rough draft for an outline has been assembled simply by doing a Find search for the thematic keywords. In this way, the rough outline documents how the theme is being developed (or in what ways it has been left underdeveloped) in the manuscript *currently*. When I revise the outline, I'll be planning what to do next—how to develop the themes more clearly and powerfully over the course of the story, and how to use what I will then know about the themes of my work to revise the character arcs and the plot.

This first run of the outline merely documents what is happening in the manuscript right now. Take a look at it. What do you notice? As you note each "touch" on the theme, each plucking of that chord, as the outline leaps from chapter to chapter, where does that theme appear to gain melody, resonance, and power? Where does it feel a bit flat? Are there long stretches between mentions of the theme? Where does it need to appear more frequently or prominently? Are there missed opportunities?

Example: First Draft of Thematic Outline for *By a Slender Thread*

Keywords: Thread; labyrinth

1. Chapter 1 – Regina briefly, in the first paragraph, imagines the alleys of Rome as a zombie-infested "labyrinth."

2. Chapter 2 – Marcus shares the Greek tale of Theseus and the labyrinth with the reader, offering a narrative that the characters will continue to refer back to, in different ways, throughout the novel: "When Marcus was a child, his Greek nurse had sung him songs about a sea king who lived in a palace. On the walls were

frescoes of dolphins that bore men to safety and sirens
that drowned them. There were windows wide like
flared nostrils through which the palace sucked in the
brined breath of the ocean. The Minoan king sat on a
high seat as the palace's brain, and behind him in a
luxurious bed rested his wife, its heart. Deep in the
earth beneath, his architect had wound the tangled
intestinal tunnels of the palace, a labyrinth without
light, without clean air, without exit or egress. In those
bowels he'd cast the kingdom's undigested refuse:
human sacrifices swallowed whole, virgins shoved into
the pits that were the palace's belly, the architect
himself devoured by his own creation. And in the
deepest and most constipated region, breathing in its
own stench and shit and sweat, lurked the queen's half-
animal son. The son's bellowing trembled the walls of
the labyrinth and rose like heartburn in the night to
trouble the queen's sleep. But besides the beast's
moans and the virgins' screams, and the dry weeping of
old Daedalus, nothing was ever vomited back up.
Nothing escaped. ...Inescapable as that labyrinth was,
it was a mere shadow on a cave wall; in Rome, the
more gruesome reality was the ghetto at the bottom of
the hills, into which all the city's sewage gurgled its way
toward a river that stank. The few public fountains
were surrounded at all hours by sickly citizens with clay
jars slimed from much use, pushing against each other
to get a few drops of the water leaking from the marble
mouths of lecherous satyrs or from between the thighs
of a nymph. The water was this labyrinth's one clean
thing, carried down in streams from forever-winter
peaks, then down the long, high aqueducts. But the
water flowed over many dirty hands and backs in the
hourly chaos at each fountain. Elsewhere in this human

maze, old men and women lay neglected, festering slowly on filthy beds in high tenements." A few moments later, Marcus compares himself (unfavorably) to the legendary hero, Theseus: "He glanced down at Ariadne, who gazed back at him with wide eyes, and he recalled those songs his Achaian nurse used to recite for him when he was small. Theseus had been lost in a labyrinth, too, in danger of being eaten – and there had been an Ariadne in *that* story, who'd shown the hero the way out. Short and lean within his brown, Suburan tunic, Marcus did not feel much like bronze-limbed Theseus striding out to do battle with monsters of the ancient world and to claim for himself fortune and a parentage both ancient and unexpected."

3. Chapter 3 – Regina is in her fever after giving hundreds of the dead peace at the end of Chapter 1; in her delirium, she is lost among their terrible memories. Sabra says Regina is "lost in a labyrinth of her own making; only by a slender thread can she be guided out." Sabra also describes her own body as fraying with age; "some morning soon I will wake up and be nothing but a pile of thin, tattered threads."

4. Chapter 7 – Trajan thinks of duty in terms of the thread and the labyrinth: "Duty was ever the slender thread he unspooled and then followed back through the fogs of the Roman world."

5. Chapter 9 – Marcus thinks of the fragility of life (its thread easily snipped by the Fates) in terms of the slender thread: "But he was spent. She was spent. They lay together against the wall of the Life Gate, clinging to each other and clinging to life, which seemed such a

slender thread in their hands, so easily frayed, so easily cut."

6. Chapter 10: As the refugees are near despair, Ariadne tells the story of the Athenians and the slender thread: "There were men conspiring against the city, and when they failed, they retreated to the temple of Athena and sought sanctuary there. The men of the city urged them to come out to stand trial. And they were so afraid, they tied a thread around the wrist of the goddess, a long thread that they unspooled like a man's life as they left the temple. But the thread was slender and tied around Athena's hand not by her choice but by theirs, and as they passed the temple to the Kindly Ones, it snapped. The men of Athens saw the thread break and fell on the conspirators with stones, with rocks hurled in the air! They knew the goddess had abandoned them. That is what you think has happened here, isn't it? You think that. The thread that ties us to God's hand has snapped, and all that remains is for Atropos to snip the thousand threads of our lives, and for us to fall moaning into Hades. That's what you think." She adds: "Father Polycarp told me that his God has tied such a slender thread to each of our hearts. It *is* slender, like Athena's, and only in the brightest sunlight can you even see it. But that thread is tied by his will, not our own. That thread is soaked in his own blood, for God who loves us has bled for us, and that blood has made the thread strong, so strong not even Atropos with her shears of silver can cut it. Nothing can cut it, this new thread, this scarlet cord. Not death, not anything in life, not the fury of the gods nor the savagery of the spirits below. It will continue unspooling over the highest peak or through the deepest pit. Nothing can sever this thread that binds us to God's hand. Nothing but our

choice if we let it go, for God will never let it go. Hold to Father Polycarp's hope, all of you. Never let go. We are still here. Many are dead, we have lost *so* many—" Now her voice had become thick with tears. –"But *we are still here.* We still breathe. We still hold our end of God's thread. Hold on. *Hold on.* Never let go."

7. Chapter 18: Poor Marcus! "Polycarp's God died with him. And my fathers' gods are sleeping in their tombs. Libya is right: our traditions are an ungodded labyrinth with only monsters in the middle."

8. Chapter 24: Regina Romae leads the refugees out of a burning Rome with a slender thread, holding one end and guiding them all to safety.

That last scene occurs at the midway point in the story. I have hastily sketched notes about later scenes in the book:

- Priscilla, Marcus's love interest, winds a slender thread about one of her wrists and one of his on one crucial night, binding her hand to his.
- There may be a scene in which Regina looks up at the sky and sees just wisps of cloud like unspooled thread, at a moment when she fears that all threads have come undone and that they are lost. She will have to learn or relearn what she is holding onto.

But for now, let's just take a good look at this first *half* of an outline and see what we can uncover about this story that may prove useful for revising and intensifying it.

2. ANALYSIS:
EXPLORING THE GAPS

Now that I have this partial outline that documents where my theme is appearing in the current rough draft of the manuscript, I can ask myself some sharp questions. If *never let go [of the slender thread of hope]* is the thematic keynote of the novel, I can look for opportunities I haven't written yet to dramatize that idea of *not* letting go, and I can look at those scenes I've written already and locate missed opportunities there. And besides showing me where to heighten the thematic intensity of my fiction, a thematic outline can also reveal where I have wandered off-topic or off-track for too many scenes.

When you're looking over a thematic outline, you want to do two things:

1. Note where in your story the metaphor that's central to your theme appears to be missing or absent.

2. Brainstorm at least one opportunity to add it in each of those gaps, in a meaningful way that comments on the story's conflict or precipitates the next stage of the conflict.

How might we do that with my own thematic outline, shared above? What did *you* notice about it? Here are a few things I just noted about it:

1. The brief mention in the first chapter—of Rome becoming labyrinthine—is a bit weak. The metaphor is really developed in the second chapter, but there is a missed opportunity to make it central to the opening of the story.

   One such opportunity: Since the *slender thread* will become so key to Regina's choices later in the story, perhaps here, at the outset, she could be thinking of how ill-prepared she is to unspool such a thread across the devastated streets of Rome, how desperately she is trying to guide refugees out, how much she wishes Polycarp was here to offer *her* a thread to cling to, a way out of the maze.

   Better yet, the child she saves in this opening scene could be linked directly to the image of the thread. Perhaps when the child fled to the back of the insula, string trailed behind her, and Regina follows it to find her. Or maybe a thread or string is all the orphaned child has left of her father, all she was able to clutch in her hand as she was pulled away.

   In either case, the image of the thread needs to be immediate, present, and poignant in this first scene.

2. After Chapter 3, there are multiple chapters (in fact, some forty or fifty pages) where Things

Happen in the plot but the theme appears largely forgotten and unmentioned. Yet this early section of the book is an especially critical time to develop the theme, and upon a closer look, those chapters may present opportunities to add layers to the metaphors either of the labyrinth or the slender thread.

One such opportunity: In these intermediary chapters, there are descriptions of the refuge Regina's people have made (before it is burned in Chapter 6). Regina believes in the craft of peacemaking as a kind of weaving (Greek *eirenepoein*); this could be a perfect time to touch briefly on how a healthy community is one where the threads of all those individual lives are woven together, none left out. This can be contrasted with Roman ideals of hierarchy and order (Roman *pax* or peace as a disciplined state).

Another opportunity: The refugees are dealing with so much death and loss. There could be mention of the Fates snipping the thread of life too often. I could make the imagery cold and brutal (*shearing the thread each time the dead rip into a man's gut with their red fingers*)—or sad (*so many threads falling to the ground, to lie in heaps, rubbish forgotten by the gods*)—or both.

3. In Chapter 18, Marcus alludes to Libya's belief that the world is an ungodded labyrinth, but I've

never written any such lines for Libya. I need to add those!

4. None of the scenes in which characters confront their antagonists (e.g., Regina vs Emperor Domitian, Regina vs Trajan) appear on the rough draft of this thematic outline, indicating that none of them have the thematic thread woven through them (yet). That's a problem. No wonder I've been at a loss as to how best to handle these high-stakes, pivotal scenes!

One such opportunity: There are endless options for this one, and I will need to do some scribbling to see which spark excitement on the page. I could compare (from Regina's perspective) her following the slender thread of faith to Trajan pulling himself and his men along the heavy cord of duty. Perhaps Trajan speaks of wishing he could cut through the tangle of his duties like Alexander through the Gordian knot. "Kill or be killed," he mutters. "In battle, matters are simple. After the battle, they are not." How Regina responds at this moment may give the reader (and me!) some important clues. Does she admire Trajan's commitment to his duty? Is she saddened by it? Both? Does he remind her of Polycarp, carrying the heavy but freely accepted burden of his responsibilities? Or does he strike her as very different from Polycarp? How Regina responds in that moment may reveal a lot about her character, about how she sees Polycarp's servant-leadership and Trajan's warrior-leadership, and how *she* imagines leading and serving the shattered people who look to her.

Another opportunity: When Regina confronts Domitian Caesar, perhaps 'thread' comes up in the dialogue, or perhaps she has a momentary vision of mad Domitian bound tightly in dark threads, threads not the wild red hue of faith or the crimson of the blood of Jesu, but black, the color of soot and smoke and of rotting things, the hue that has overtaken Rome. Maybe when she later speaks with Trajan in his tent and the legate mentions the cord of duty, she realizes that his duty was the black thread she saw wrapped around the emperor—a cord that binds and makes captives of them all. And she realizes that it is not *duty*, whatever Trajan may think, but only the malice of a frightened old man by which they are all entrapped. Regina has thought of the *slender thread* of faith as a fragile thing that you mustn't let go of lest you get lost in the nightmare. But when she speaks with Trajan, does she then, for a brief moment, perceive the thread not as a fragile thing but as a *light* thing, a burden easier to carry than Trajan's heavy cord, a thread that you can follow by consent but that could never bind you—a thread weak enough for you to snap through if it tried to bind itself around you like the emperor's black bonds, yet strong enough to extend through the smoke and over the far horizon?

On the first page of this book, I suggested that theme, while less talked about than character or plot, in certain ways provides a writer with the most opportunities for play—for creativity, for making wild and unexpected connections, for dancing on the ink-strewn pages of your manuscript. Do you see now why I said that?

Now take note of *how* I'm brainstorming these opportunities. It's all in the wondering and the wandering—the questions you can ask yourself, in play, to start coming up with angles on a theme or a character that you haven't seen yet. Here are examples of questions that can yield a brainstorm like the one above:

- How might my thematic image look different to different characters? (e.g., for Regina and Marcus, the thread helps you *escape* the labyrinth, as it did for Theseus, but for Trajan and Domitian, the thread *binds*. Your thematic image can take on different and even opposite meanings depending on which characters are looking at it.)

- Can I raise a question about my theme in one scene and then answer it (partially) in a later scene with the same character? (e.g., Marcus, when we first meet him, wonders if he is traveling through a labyrinth in which heroes might be found; by Chapter 18, he sees it as a labyrinth in which only monsters might be found.)

- Do I get more mileage out of having the answer they come up with in that second scene be true, partially true, or false? (e.g., In Chapter 18, is Marcus correct about the ungodded labyrinth, or is he misled by his horror? Is this his low point in the story that he'll need to climb out of?)

- To what degree do I want the reader to see the thematic image the same way the character sees it, in any given scene? (Should the reader be as close to despair as Marcus, so that his climb out of that trough is also the reader's climb, stirring them to sudden joy? Or, should the reader be more hopeful than Marcus, so that they are shouting at the page, "Come on, Marcus! Don't give up! You can *do* this!")

- What kind of emotional journey do I want the *reader* to go on? Each of the two examples in the previous bullet point could involve an exciting emotional journey for the reader. In the first example, where we strive to bring the reader close to despair along with the character, we would plunge the reader into a dark place and then rescue them from that labyrinth. This makes the reader a co-sufferer and fellow hero along with the characters. In the second example, we would focus on creating just the right amount of tension between the reader's perspective and the characters', and then having the characters make the right choices *despite* their growing despair, so that the reader becomes their cheerleader.

- How can I use the language and imagery of my theme to sweep the reader along on that specific emotional journey?

- In a pivotal scene, what are all the ways I can think of to bring the thematic image in *literally*, as an actual object or apparition in the scene? What are all the ways I can think of to bring the thematic image in *metaphorically*, in either the dialogue, the narration, or the character's introspection during that scene? Which serves my purpose best? Or, can I do both at the same time? Does that overload the reader to the point of hitting them over the head with the image, or do I think I can pull it off, like a series of drumbeats that increase the reader's excitement, anxiety, or curiosity? In Chapter 1 above, we could bring the thematic image in *literally* by having the child grasp a string or a handful of frayed threads, all she was able to tear from her father's garment when separated from him. We can bring the thematic image in *metaphorically* by having Regina long for an unfrayed thread to follow out of the labyrinth, or by a reference to the snipping of the father's life thread by the Fates or by the cruelty of Rome.

These are examples of the types of questions you can ask to get yourself brainstorming what unseen opportunities you have. Once you have several opportunities to consider, the next three questions are always the same:

1. What effect does each of these opportunities achieve? (That is, what emotional experience does each create, and how does each of these opportunities build on the themes and tensions in your story?)
2. What effect do I *need* to achieve in this scene, or at this stage of the story?

3.   Which opportunity best achieves this effect?

If none of the ideas you came up with do a very good at achieving the desired effect, then take a breath and check to see if either (a) you are looking for the wrong effect after all (sometimes our subconscious is a lot smarter than we are, and tosses ideas our way that don't fit what we think we *want* to do but instead fit what we *need* to do at this point in the story), or if (b) you simply need to brainstorm more ideas, this time with a clearer sense of what kind of experience you hope to evoke in this scene or chapter.

Exercise 23

Brainstorm two more opportunities that *you* see to fill one or more of the four gaps I noted in my sample thematic outline from *By a Slender Thread*. To do this, use what you know so far about the story, its themes, and its characters— and refer as needed to the sample questions in the bullet list over the previous three pages—but imagine yourself the writer, taking the story where you please.

In this case, you're using my sample story and outline as a playground and proving ground to practice your skill at thematic outlining and at spotting and evaluating unexpected opportunities. Later, in Exercises 24-26, you'll do this with *your* story and your thematic outline.

This is the kind of brainstorming you'll want to do—and that you *can* do—when you start to construct a thematic outline. This type of brainstorming opens up more exciting possibilities for your story, often possibilities you hadn't suspected or imagined yet.

3. REVISION: MAKING THE OUTLINE FUNCTIONAL

All right, let's bring order to this delicious chaos. We started with a Find/Search that just surfaced a list of moments where the thematic concerns of the book are already either deliberately commented on or alluded to in the draft. That just gives us a list of scenes. Now, to translate this into an actual and functional *thematic outline*, let's divide the outline into several sections and label them; each section represents a 'stage' in the author's presentation of the story's main theme.

For example, if the novel will not be 100% definitive in answering the question, then we might label several sections as follows:

1. Raising the Question
2. Complicating the Question
3. Tentatively Answering the Question
4. Demolishing that Answer We Thought We Had
5. Looking at the Question in a New Light
6. Giving the Question Back to the Reader.

Remember that you are inviting the reader on an adventure, no less than your character.

A different outline may have different stages. Maybe a different book follows the outline of:

1. Raising the Question
2. Complicating the Question
3. Finding the Answer
4. Doubting the Answer
5. Learning the Answer Really Can Be Trusted

That's a frequent outline for romances and love stories, for example.

Next, we need to:

1. Identify where the transitions between stages happen in your story (and make those moments tense and exciting).
2. For each scene within each stage, note a specific example of how you can develop the theme.

Example: Second Draft of Thematic Outline for *By a Slender Thread*

Chapters 1-3: Raising the Question.

The job in this first stage is to get the reader excited about the question: Will our heroes find a slender thread to lead themselves, their people, and the reader out of what appears to be a no-win scenario, out of despair and a legacy of violence? Literally, out of the labyrinth of the hungry and monstrous dead that Rome has become—and, metaphorically, out of the labyrinth of our violent and unresolved past that still hungers to devour our lives in the present?

Chapter 1: Regina, following a thread to find a lost child and feeling the weight of all the lives depending on her to guide them out of the labyrinth, wishes someone could unspool a thread for her too, to lead her out of the labyrinth of her past and her pain.

Chapter 2: Marcus unpacks the labyrinth metaphor, wishes he was half the hero Theseus was. Tie this more explicitly to Marcus's estrangement from his family and his past.

Chapter 3: Regina is lost in a labyrinth of her own making (a labyrinth constructed to contain her trauma, as though her trauma is a monster that mustn't be faced); Sabra suggests God is lost in there with her.

Chapters 4-9: Complicating the Question:

(I) How slender is the thread, how fragile?
(II) What thread can lead us out? Duty? Faith? Love? Tradition?

(In a different kind of story, you could complicate the question by asking: *Who* can be trusted to lead us by a thread?)

In this section, I can really bring home that the dead aren't the only minotaur in the labyrinth; the traditions of our past must be escaped too; the story of faith, hope, love, and peace that can trace a path for us into the future is a slender thread, difficult to find, difficult to follow, difficult to hold to in the dark.

Chapter 4: As fire starts in the city and approaches the refuge, there's a scene where Regina faces one of the

119

hungry dead at the door and finds the soul of the person that corpse used to be, and gives him rest. Bring in the language of the 'thread' here: looking inside the dead man and finding the snipped ends of his life's thread. Are they truly severed, or can those ends yet be tied together? Can the man be led out and free of that hungry corpse, that ruin of the past?

Chapter 5: Imagery of a labyrinth in flames. The fire itself is the monster at the heart of the labyrinth now, something hungrier than the dead. Something in which all threads might wither.

Chapter 6: When the volunteer firefighters, buying Regina time, get overwhelmed by the fire, their hair becomes burning threads. Or some image of that kind.

Chapter 7: Trajan follows the thread of duty through Rome's darkest night, and that thread does not snap— but as he makes choices that appall him, the thread starts to feel more like a strangling cord than a way out of his labyrinth.

Chapter 8: Night in the Colosseum, where the refugees have taken shelter. Marcus holds Pris, a woman who fled the flames with him, as she sleeps; he can't find any thread to hold to, but he can hold her.

Chapter 9: The moaning dead outside the Colosseum; Libya and her gladiators defending the gates; Regina's conversation with the ghost of Remus, brother of Rome's founder. For the author to decide: Does Remus speak of the thread of tradition, or perhaps of how Rome has 'lost the thread' of its story? Remus reminds Regina of how Rome was founded around the temple of

Asylum, a safe place for refugees, the place where the threads out of the labyrinth led, but now Rome has become the opposite of what it was intended to be. "You are the only one left here who has my brother's heart," Remus tells Regina. "In his own city, only you are left." She says, "I'm not from this city." He answers, "But it is *your* city, isn't it? And haven't you been listening? Neither was he. Nor any who came here to Asylum on Rome's first hill. I hear you do not like the Roman gods, but that your own watches over fugitives, over men and women without homes. That is Roman enough for me."

Chapters 10-16: Tentatively Answering the Question:

Hold on to that slender thread of faith. Never let go.

Chapter 10: Ariadne's impassioned speech to the other refugees about how if God holds the thread rather than we, then we can trust that thread will hold, as long as we hold to *it*.

Chapter 11: Told through Marcus's point of view, the venture to the Baths of Titus in search of fresh water. Rome, once so familiar, is now a labyrinth of corpses and scorched marble, yet strangely beautiful in the sunlight. The Baths of Titus are a worse labyrinth, dark and possibly full of the dead. For the author to figure out: How will the theme and the thematic imagery of the 'slender thread' work in this scene? Is the thread literal (do they tie a rope or string between the different adventurers to keep from getting separated?) Is the thread figurative (does Regina's voice, calling or singing softly ahead of them, serve as the thread they follow)? Is the thread purely symbolic (some thread within himself that Marcus is holding onto)? Or, is Marcus the one person who doubts the thread at this point, who can't find the thread to follow? When he saves Pris in the darkness, is he *her* thread? Does her faith in him become his thread? Do I entice the story into a romantic direction at this point?

And so on…

There, you see? Now I am asking the kind of questions that can empower me to both refine and deepen the plot. While Ariadne comes into her own as a religious leader and as the wonder-worker Regina's disciple and sister, leading Rome's survivors by the slender thread of *faith*, at the same time, a plotline might develop with Marcus and Priscilla, where the slender thread that leads you out is *love*. As an author, I can play with how I bounce those two pairs off of each other. I can ask myself if I want a 'love triangle' between Marcus, Ariadne, and Priscilla. Or perhaps I find the love triangle option juvenile and unfulfilling, and instead I want to compare and contrast how two pairs of characters—Regina and Ariadne, Marcus and Priscilla—find ways to strengthen each other. Maybe I want to say that a slender thread cannot be followed out of the labyrinth by yourself; it is community that saves us. (Theseus, after all, didn't come up with that slender thread by himself.) If that is the case, maybe I want to do more to emphasize how Regina has been isolated by her trauma and how Marcus has been isolated by his rejection of his oppressive patrician family and their tradition, and the emotional and relational drama that is threaded throughout this dark tale of survival is a drama of how Regina and Marcus each repair that isolation, how they each accept that they can't do this alone, and how each of them, after great suffering, find healthy ways to trust others.

The thematic outline can help me choose from among the specific directions I could take as I finish this novel— and can help me refine the direction I'm taking. It can focus my effort and keep me from trying to write ten novels in one manuscript.

4. USING YOUR THEMATIC OUTLINE TO DEVELOP CHARACTER AND HONE PLOT

Let's talk more about *how* to use this outline as a tool. If you've read my book *Write Characters Your Readers Won't Forget*, this is when you would refer back to your character arc. The thematic outline and the character arc: These two tools sharpen each other. That's because:

- Identifying the stages on your thematic outline can help you clarify the choices your character has to make—and what is at stake in those choices.

- Identifying the scenes of critical choice on the character arc can help you adjust the pacing on your thematic outline—where to go *subtle* and where to go *overt*, and what things need to be said or shown about your theme before you get to that next critical moment of choice for the character.

If you haven't read *Write Characters Your Readers Won't Forget*, here's the quick version, the five-minute crash course:

A character arc is an outline that consists of between four and seven scenes, in which each scene is a moment of critical realization for the character, where a character-defining choice is either made or postponed. These moments of choice are how the character becomes who they are at the end of the story. For each moment of choice on your outline, you identify:

- What the character desires in that moment
- What fear they are facing
- What wound from their past is shaping the specific ways in which they choose to face (or not face) that fear
- What the choice they make costs them.

Then, you identify, for each of those critical moments of choice:

- What does the reader need to know, feel, or realize before getting to this moment?
- What does the character need to know, feel, or realize prior to this moment?
- What does my character (and my reader) need to experience or encounter in order to know, feel, or realize those things?

The answers to those three questions empower you to reshape and refine your plot. They give you the bare minimum of what *has* to be in your story in between the 4-7 scenes that make up the character arc. That tells you:

- Where your story may be bogging down in material that doesn't actually move us toward the next character arc scene.
- Where critical material is missing.
- Which material in your story—which moments, which scenes, which information—is essential and most worthy of emphasis.

It helps you spot those scenes where you need to ramp up the intensity in order to prepare the way for the choices your character has to make.

The choices are what make us love your character and their story. The plot is how you get us to those choices and how you show us the consequences of those choices. The theme is how you demonstrate why those choices matter, and how *much* they matter.

If I set the character arc beside the working draft of a thematic outline, I can see where to tighten the story further. For example, let's look at the most critical character arc in *By a Slender Thread*: Regina's. After the death of her mentor, Regina believes that she has to carry everything—and everyone—by herself. We see her repeatedly making the same choice, taking on more of the weight, at greater and greater cost to herself. Her ghosts get louder and louder in her mind, and the strain this woman feels as she tries to lead thousands of refugees across zombie-infested ancient Italy is considerable:

Regina's Character Arc

Scene 1: In that first chapter, "Mater Romae," Regina encounters a man from her own homeland and promises to protect his daughter—a young Syrian girl who reminds her of herself as a child—and by extension, she is vowing to protect all the survivors. To be Mother to Rome the way Polycarp, her mentor, was Father. She accepts the burden.

Scene 2: Waking from the nightmare-dreams into which the act of granting rest to dozens of the dead had cast her, Regina rises from her sickbed to find Rome in flames and the dead at the door. Shaking under the burden and freshly, acutely aware of its cost to her, she still chooses to go to the door and free the dead. This happens in Chapter 4.

Scene 3: Regina's first real moment of despair—as she gazes out from the wall of the Colosseum at an ashen Rome packed with the hungry dead. Behind her are the survivors, trusting her to lead them. She nearly breaks at the top of that wall. This is the scene in which she encounters the ghost of Remus.

Scene 4: Regina springs to action, grasping the slender thread of faith tightly, and she leads thousands of the living out of Rome, all of them following that thread behind her. She sings as she leads them down the Appian Way.

Scene 5: After the child Regina promised to protect dies, she breaks. She gets lost, weeping, in the labyrinth of her past, where all her ghosts clamor to devour her spirit.

Scene 6: In the closing chapter of the book, Regina leads the survivors into their final escape, holding that slender thread and singing as she performs a miracle. This time, her friends—Ariadne, Marcus, Libya—are walking right beside her, sharing their strength. She carries a child in her arms: either the Syrian girl resurrected, or someone else's child. She couldn't save everyone—she has to come to terms with that—but she can save *this* child, this one, now, tonight, and any others who will follow her. With that slender thread in her fingers, and looking ahead into the dark, she feels, at last, real hope.

On this arc, Scene 3 will need to prepare the reader for Scene 5, by showing us what it would be like if Regina broke, prior to the scene when she does break. This creates an expectation and a pleasant dread for the reader, who begins to anticipate and fear the moment when Regina *will* break. Perhaps the encounter with the ghost of Remus pulls her back from the brink—or more likely, what pulls her back is something her friend Ariadne says to her or does for her, in a scene that takes something Remus said and makes it feel real to her (and the reader) in a more immediate and eventually painful way. Perhaps Ariadne stepping in and making that speech to the refugees and organizing, on the fly, a sisterhood of women to help is the first moment when Regina dares to believe that she doesn't have to carry it *all*, by herself. Possibly she feels that Ariadne has thrown *her* a thread to hold onto, in that moment.

Similarly, Scene 4—when Regina leads the refugees out of Rome—needs to prepare us for Scene 6, which will be the same type of act on a larger scale, more triumphantly and with more hope. The differences between these two scenes need to be clear to me as I write them, too. In Scene 4, Regina leads the survivors alone, and she feels her aloneness keenly, and it's all she can do to *keep* walking; Marcus and Ariadne look to her almost worshipfully in that scene, and their worship feels like a burden to Regina. In Scene 6, they walk together as brothers and sisters, and that is why she is able to do what she does, and able to walk with the ghosts of her past all about her and not break in fear or fatigue.

Looking at this character arc and at the thematic outline, I can see things that need doing. For example, I need to clarify and heighten the emotional and thematic impact of that encounter with the ghostly revenant of Remus, and make sure what is said during that encounter speaks directly to Regina's fears and hopes. I also need to tie the imagery of the labyrinth to the *past*, very clearly, both for Regina and Marcus. In my existing draft of the manuscript, the thematic keyword of the labyrinth refers usually, mostly, to the literal, physical maze of a devastated Rome. But that is only the most superficial layer of the labyrinth my characters are striving to escape. What I need to do, in revising these early chapters, is really give the reader some haunting moments where we are aware of the horrors lurking in that labyrinth of the past—for Regina, a past filled with pain, where violence is the monster, and for Marcus, a past filled with emptiness, where tradition is the monster. In both cases, that labyrinth needs to be terrifying to the characters and to the reader. We have to *feel* how urgently, how badly these characters want to find the thread that will lead them out. That emotional urgency mustn't get lost amid writing all the action and momentum and survival-urgency of the zombie story. Instead, that emotional urgency must be the *most* present on the page; it is what gives the story its meaning and its flavor. It's what charges the events of the plot with their emotional intensity.

When I write out Marcus's character arc, I need to ensure the labyrinth is just as scary for him as Regina's is for her. It's a different fear; he and Regina, the two disciples of deceased Father Polycarp, enter the story from opposite directions. Regina is a manumitted slave, abducted from her homeland as a child and sold, someone who had never had anything until she met Polycarp. Marcus is the son of a Roman patrician, raised in luxury, until on a night of debauchery he got lost in the Subura—Rome's poorest district—and encountered starving children, realizing in one harrowing moment that although he had everything, it meant *nothing*; his life was empty until he met Polycarp. My task as a writer is to play up these differences and show how the two bounce off of each other in the story. And maybe there is also something about both of their labyrinths that is the same: maybe the monster at the center of both mazes, the fear, is in both cases the dread that they won't be able to help others who are suffering. Maybe each of them feels that if they can save one person, their life will have meaning and value. For Regina, that one person is the Syrian child, who needn't suffer as she did; for Marcus, perhaps that one person is Priscilla, an ex-patrician like himself who now has no one and nothing and will starve if left alone in the ghoul-haunted wasteland Rome has become. For both Regina and Marcus, the life they have to save—the one whose hand might hold the thread leading them (they hope) out of their labyrinth—is someone who reminds them of their younger selves.

That's a lot I can play with in a story, now that I'm *aware* of it and planning for it! Now my task is to go back and revise those early scenes so that all the seeds of this are planted, and so that the first time the labyrinth metaphor comes up in the story, it is harrowing—and suggestive of so much more than just the physical realities of this collapsing Rome, as was the case in the first draft.

I have a clearer sense now of *why* this story matters to its specific characters (and of why it matters to *me*) and, at last, I can see the patterns in the story. The threads. Now I can do the work to really weave this tale.

In this way, the character arc and the thematic outline are both tools for taking the invisible, perhaps barely-there threads in your narrative and making them suddenly, blindingly visible to you, in all their beauty and potential. When that occurs, it's an incredible moment for a writer. Granted, you usually emerge from that moment with a *lot* of work to do—but, in and after that moment (or moments) of epiphany, your story is beautiful and passionate enough to be worthy of that work. And perhaps, in doing the work, you, the craftsman, become worthy of your story.

Exercise 24

Return to one of the thematic questions you identified in Exercise 7 and to the keyword and image you experimented with in Exercises 18 and 19. Create a thematic outline, tracking the occurrences of that thematic keyword and image throughout your manuscript. If either your manuscript is in a very early state or if you already have ideas about how you might revise the thematic thread in your story, then create a thematic outline that tracks where you think the thematic keyword or imagery might or should occur in your story. In what scenes will it appear, and what layers of meaning or emotion will be added to it in each of those scenes?

Exercise 25

Now create a character arc for your protagonist or for another principal character whose journey through the story you would like to examine more closely. Identify several scenes of critical choices that may change how your character conceives of their identity and agency in the story. For each character arc scene, identify:

- What the character desires in that moment
- What fear they are facing
- What wound from their past is shaping the specific ways in which they choose to face (or not face) that fear
- What the choice they make costs them

Then, identify for each of these scenes:

- How does this choice reinforce, complicate, or otherwise interact with the thematic question at the heart of your story?
- In what ways does your thematic keyword or imagery appear in this scene? In what ways *could* it? What are

your best opportunities to wield that imagery in a way that makes this scene of critical, character-defining choice more tense and meaningful? What are your best opportunities to wield that imagery in ways that clarify and heighten what's at stake for your characters at this moment of choice?

Exercise 26

Now compare your thematic outline and your character arc and consider the shape of your plot, or the shape your plot might take. Based on what you see on these two outlines, identify three opportunities to add, subtract, or rearrange scenes to snap your themes into sharper focus and render the character's key moments of choice (and the buildup to those scenes) more intense.

WHEN TO CREATE YOUR THEMATIC OUTLINE

The two partial outlines I shared earlier in this chapter— the first draft of a thematic outline and its revision—map out only the first half of the novel, if that. Having a third or half of a longer story written is actually a fantastic time to do a thematic outline and a character arc, because these activities can clarify a lot of what's going on in your story for you, and then you can proceed with the rest of your draft in a more planful way. Many (though not all) writers find it useful to permit themselves a little wandering and wondering early in the process of writing a long story, because the fortuitous discoveries made while still getting to know your story are often what ultimately bring the tale to life. It's when you meet the most interesting characters and find the most riveting scenes. At the one-third or halfway mark, though, once you have some ideas about who your characters really are and what matters to them, it's time to buckle down and have the relationship talk with your novel or script: Where are we going, and what kind of story are we living together?

In writing classes and at writers' conferences, there is often a lot of talk about whether a writer is a *pantser* or a *plotter*. The plotter has elaborate synopses and outlines everything from the start; the pantser leaps in without an outline and just goes with the flow. Focusing on thematic outlines and character arcs rather than devising a plot synopsis allows you to act as both, tap the strengths of each, and operate from both positions at once—embracing both the joy of spontaneous discovery in your story, *and* the rigor of planning ahead.

TWO WORDS OF CAUTION

Two quick bits of advice, however:

1. Your thematic outline is a tool, not a prescription.
2. Don't get lost in the weeds at the expense of your *story*.

If you sit down and write out a thematic outline, it's imperative that you don't allow it to become a restrictive device. It mustn't constrain or imprison your creativity; it is a tool that you can use judiciously to ignite your creativity. It is intended as a slender thread to help you navigate through the labyrinth of your draft, not as a bit of rope to tie your hands.

What I mean by this is that your thematic outline should evolve and change as you discover or test things about your story (just as in the examples I shared from *By a Slender Thread* above). It's meant to provide you with a map of something that's happening in your story—a map of something wonderful—but it's a magical map that you can alter at each step, as you discover more exciting ways to develop your story.

Similarly, there's a danger in adopting too mechanical of an approach to your thematic outline. If you dive in too early—before you've written down enough of your story to provide the kind of raw material and insight into your characters and their world that makes a thematic outline useful—you can find yourself simply jotting down a prescription for how a given image or metaphor will appear in each scene in the book, in a way that replaces the living organism of your story with a robot. Generally speaking, if you write down a thematic outline and find that it inspires you to revise scenes and to add new ones or new bits of dialogue that you'd never thought of before, and if these new ideas are more exciting to you than daunting, then the tool is serving its purpose. If, instead, it feels like drudgery, then pause, step back, and figure out why. It may be that your themes aren't clear enough to you yet. Or it may be that you aren't sure what keywords and images really capture *your* imagination. It may be that you have four or five, or twenty, possibilities in your manuscript, and the one you've focused on and started to outline is the wrong one—that is, not the one that is actually most compelling to you.

If you find that this is the case, then return to Exercises 18 and 19, which you can find in Chapter 4. Exercise 18 empowers you to brainstorm the imagery that really captures and displays your thematic question in a way that excites you. Exercise 19 is a way to take that imagery and brainstorm how it might appear in 10 scenes over the course of a story. These are good steps to take prior to a full thematic outline of your manuscript, because these initial steps allow you to define and test what excites you most in your story. If you can weave an image through ten scenes and get excited about it and energized, then you have something worth outlining on a larger scale.

THE GOAL OF THE THEMATIC OUTLINE

Some first drafts simply lack material—scenes, dialogue, even supporting characters—that would make the story truly powerful, that would allow you to develop your story into the most evocative and riveting version of itself. Other drafts have so much extraneous material, so much clutter, that the material that really *matters* gets buried. Depending on which of these best describes the situation with your manuscript, your goal in embarking on a thematic outline may be either to find out what's *missing*, which you can add in order to really heighten the emotional intensity of your story—or to find out what's most *essential*, so that you can focus on it and sweep some of the clutter out of its way.

Every writer is different. In my own case, I typically am *missing* material early in my process. Clutter isn't the issue; the issue is adding in the material that will really make the story powerful. In one egregious example, when I did a character arc and thematic outline for my third novel, *Strangers in the Land*, I found that I was missing a character! For those who have read the novel, the character was Hurriya—which may surprise you, as Devora's relationship with Hurriya is the most important in the novel. In the first draft, Hurriya didn't exist. I found her because when I mapped out Devora's character arc and a thematic outline on the topic of *strangers in the land*, I saw at once that in order for my protagonist's relinquishing of her own xenophobia and her choice to fight for *all* the people in the land to be as powerful and heartwrenching as I wanted it to be, I needed to write in a character who was one of the 'strangers in the land,' and to whom, from her perspective, my protagonist was a stranger in the land. Their journey from being enemies to being kin would be the defining journey of the story.

Discovering that I literally had a *missing character* was simultaneously dismaying and exhilarating. It was dismaying because I knew immediately it would mean another six months of revision. There were a lot of scenes that needed to be added or revised. I had a lot of work to do. But it was exhilarating too, because in the moment I discovered that Hurriya needed to be in the story, entire scenes started to spring into my mind, and I realized I could push the main character farther than I had before. What's more, this new character would be exciting to write.

The work I did paid off, too. The novel came out to rave reviews, and the work I did in and because of that thematic outline and character arc prepared me to go on to write much more complex stories, with larger casts of characters and more dramatic tension in those characters' relationships. I grew as a writer.

That is the goal here: to grow your craft, to become capable of writing scenes you couldn't before and of telling stories that are more exciting, emotional, and profound than you previously believed possible. That is worth the extra six months. Try a thematic outline and see what new opportunities for storytelling, character development, and scenecraft you can find.

In the next chapter, I'll present specific, practical techniques for using your new awareness of your book's thematic threads to make the beginning, middle, and ending of your book more exciting and emotionally impactful.

6 | MASTERING BEGINNINGS, MIDDLES, AND ENDS

THIS FINAL CHAPTER ISN'T MEANT TO BE prescriptive (telling you things you *should* do) but descriptive (sharing things you *can* do). I hope that reading these ideas may help spark additional, different ideas of your own.

A way to think of the beginning of your story is that it is when you toss the thematic question to the character and to the reader. The middle is when you show off, demonstrating just how entertaining a performance of that thematic question can be. And the end is when you and the protagonist press the question firmly into the palm of the reader's hand, leaving it in their care, having either suggested an answer to it or having raised enough provocative considerations that the reader will continue wrestling with it after closing the book. In other words, your thematic outline can be a device for shaping and crafting your plot.

So let's talk about beginnings.

THE THRESHOLD TEXT

In *Write Worlds Your Readers Won't Forget*, I introduced you to the threshold text, which I learned from Tolkien scholar Andrew Hallam—the device by which the character steps from their home or their initial scene out into the world of the story, and by which the reader is invited out into the story with them. The crossing of the threshold is the first transition in the story, the first choice, the first risk taken. And the threshold is marked with clues that get the reader (and probably the character) asking or thinking about the thematic questions that matter to the story. That crucial opening sequence is both about *how* the story gets started and *why* it does. And, if you are working intentionally with a thematic keyword or image, this is probably when it makes a first significant appearance—even though the character and the reader won't fully grasp all the layers of that significance until later.

The threshold text presents a question; the story itself then gives an answer or presents various possible answers for the reader to deliberate between. Often, there is a literal threshold involved—a door stepped into or out of. In *The Hobbit*, this is the door of Bag End. Gandalf the wizard appears at Bilbo's door one fine morning to invite him to an adventure. Convinced that adventures are utterly nasty and uncomfortable things that make you late for dinner, Bilbo retreats into his home, refusing the adventure. Gandalf then marks a rune into Bilbo's door, as if he is marking the word *adventure* onto Bilbo's story. Dwarves will find that rune and show up insistently on

139

Bilbo's doorstep, and Bilbo will soon find himself running out that door despite himself, and will spend an entertaining novel considering the necessity of both comfort and adventure in life.

Often the rune that is marked on the door is what's missing in the character's life. Maybe that's adventure. Maybe that's love. Maybe that's simply the thrill of risk; maybe your character is in the throes of a midlife crisis. Maybe it's compassion; maybe that threshold text is the door of old Scrooge's shop, and one of his employees is hesitating before stepping through to go home, delaying a moment to ask for a holiday, for time with family. *Christmas? Compassion? Bah! Humbug!* Scrooge insists. But, just as in *The Hobbit*, wizards and Christmas ghosts and authors have a way of getting insistent with their protagonists and even of shoving them over the thresholds that they need to cross. Not all characters (nor all readers) are carried over the threshold as gently as a bride.

If you are alert to your story's thematic concerns and implications, then you can get intentional about marking the rune on your character's door, so to speak. That is, you can get deliberate and strategic about writing the thematic question into that first scene. In unforgettable stories, that question is always there—it's why the story matters to us, even at the start. We talked about this quite a bit in Chapter 1; what I want to discuss here is the technique, which is the threshold text. Come on, then—let's make a door.

Exercise 27

Take a look at the first scene in your manuscript, or, if it hasn't been written yet, take a moment and try imagining it in your head or scribbling it down on a bit of paper. What threshold might be crossed during this scene? (Or what threshold might the character fail to cross?) Reimagine this scene with a literal door. It could be the door to a home or an office. It could be a car door. The 'door' could be the cover of a diary that the character has stolen and is starting to read. Perhaps the front cover of the diary even has a door drawn *on* it. What kind of door? What color? What does the door on the cover suggest about what kind of life is inscribed within that diary, and how does the protagonist feel about that? How do they feel about the secrets they think they are about to read and discover?

Now, to select that door and to describe for yourself (as the author) what that door *means*, consider:

1. What clues does this door give the reader about the kind of story they're about to step into?
2. What does it cost the character to go through the door?
3. What is the cost of *not* going through the door?
4. How does this door (or the act of stepping through it, or what is on either side of it) frame for the reader the central thematic keyword, concept, or image?

Consider the opening scene—the prologue—of the first episode in the Netflix series *Arcane*. We first see a bridge turned into a battlefield, and two children lost in the debris. We see a warrior smashing his way through the enemy and then stopping when he sees the two crying children. He looks around at the devastation on this bridge that he'd been trying to fight his way across; he sees the body of the children's mother, slaughtered during the fight. He takes the children and walks with them, protecting them, off the bridge, retreating from his battle.

Instead of the goal on the other side of that bridge, he has chosen to protect these two orphans. The opening scene implies thematic questions—for what will we sacrifice our ideals and our goals? For what will we turn back from the battle? Or, asked the other way around, what or who are we willing to sacrifice? What costs are we actually willing to pay?

This choice between battling your way outward to achieve your warrior's goal and drawing back to protect your loved ones opens up one of the defining thematic tensions woven throughout the conflicts in the rest of the story. Implied and demonstrated visually for us in the first scene, it is stated explicitly at the end of the first chapter, by Vander, the warrior grown older, in an attempt to teach caution to one of the two children. "Who are you willing to lose?" he asks her. And that question echoes throughout the narrative. Other characters call Vander weak or a traitor when he backs down from battle with an oppressor to keep his people safe, yet he places his body between the children and harm. Silco, the villain of the story, has to choose between his nation's independence and the safety of his adopted daughter. Jayce the scientist, in one of the story's parallel plots, has to choose whether to pursue his discoveries in search of greater knowledge and greater prosperity for his nation, or bury those discoveries to prevent them from being weaponized. *Arcane* mesmerizes viewers because it has such unforgettable things to say about the cost of power and the cost of freedom, and about our yearning for justice and our yearning for family (two yearnings that may often be opposed); and because the story demands that we ask ourselves how far we would go for family. It demonstrates all of these questions in a series of betrayals and dramatic choices and tearstricken reunions that tear at our hearts even as these questions burst inside our minds like Progress Day fireworks or like Jinx's bombs.

The smoky aftermath of the battle on the bridge is a powerful threshold text to the story because all of those questions are implied by it and all of those costs are showcased in it—after all, the children's mother lies dead on the battlefield. That first opening scene dramatizes the first choice made in the story, the first answer offered to that question. Vander takes the children off the bridge; he abandons the battle to protect them. *Who are you willing to lose?* The writers of *Arcane* then return us to that same setting later in the season, providing us with a second battle on the bridge, in which the children, now several years older, are combatants. Again, we see the smoky aftermath of the battle; again, critical choices must be made.

The keyword, the thematic image, in that first scene is the *burning bridge*. Bridges are supposed to connect people, permitting us to cross over something that divides us. But this bridge has become a war zone; on it, we see the devastated aftermath of the failure to connect people. Later in the story, as law enforcers barricade the bridge, that symbol of connection is inverted yet again into a symbol of separation and of the barriers to justice and equality. While the bridge becomes a potent metaphor for what is happening on a social level in this fictional world, meanwhile, individual characters who have been separated by circumstances, by violence or by violent choices, try (and sometimes fail) to rebuild the bridges that have burned between them. Vi and Jinx, in one of several emotionally intense reunion scenes, try to mend the burned bridge between them while *on* the literal bridge in the story, a bridge that might erupt in the flames of conflict at any moment. Do you see how intricately that image of the bridge is handled, and how the threshold text uses it to set up everything that matters about the story and to thrust us, mind and heart, into the middle of the mess, the conflict, the hope and terror of this tale? The initial encounter on the bridge raises expectations and makes implicit promises to the reader about what this story will address and about what that will *feel* like to watch and experience, and the other encounters on that bridge later in the story deliver on those promises. That's the kind of storytelling you can do when you identify a clear, compelling, and emotional threshold text and then return to its imagery frequently in the story. Because *Arcane* is a dark and intense story, involving severe losses for the characters, that initial threshold is intense and devastating: dead family on a burning bridge. A different, more light-hearted tale, like *The Hobbit*, might give us a more light-hearted threshold whose risks are still real but less devastating to the reader in their implications—like the little green door that opens inward to Bilbo's home or outward to adventure.

In Chapter 4, we talked about handling thematic repetition in your story by repeating an image, each time with variation. Now we find that this image could be a setting or environment, like that bridge with its billowing smoke. Perhaps the door or the bridge, the threshold itself, becomes the metaphor you later return to throughout your narrative. Maybe your extended metaphor doesn't involve an object like a quilt or a slender thread, but a location, like a mountain cabin or the back seat of a car. Or perhaps your extended metaphor involves a repeated action performed in a specific setting, like crossing the bridge or looking into a mirror. What does your character see, each time they look into a mirror? What do they sing in their own heart, like Mulan in the Disney film, when they gaze into the mirror in the first chapter of your story, and what do they see later when they catch a glimpse of their reflection on a polished blade or on a shard of glass from a broken window? Perhaps the repeated action is a dance, and the dance at the beginning of your tale and the dance at its end look similar and maybe occur in the same location, but they *mean* different things each time.

Exercise 28

Choose a location and an action for a threshold text. What action, in what setting, could instantly ground your reader in the conflicts and thematic implications of your story? Next, come up with 5 opportunities in your story to *mirror* or repeat that action in that setting, or an action in a setting similar enough that we can easily identify it. Maybe the opening scene of your novel or script shows us the protagonist teaching their younger sibling to graffiti the side of a building, and when they are caught in the act, it precipitates a chase scene and a critical choice for the main character—abandon their sibling and run? Keep running at their sibling's pace? Turn back and risk being captured in order to create the distraction needed for their sibling to get away? Does their sibling make it home alive? Now, what are 5 ways to return to that action over the course of the story? In captivity, does your protagonist draw the same image they graffitied on the wall of that building, this time drawing it with their finger on a fogged-up bathroom mirror? Or, do they draw the image their sibling graffitied? If in this tale the society around them is becoming fascist, do they later graffiti that image on a government facility, in defiance, while robbing the facility or blowing something up? Do they graffiti that image on the sky with a floodlight, like the bat signal in *Batman*? Do they sew it on the inside of their prison uniform, as a memory to keep fighting, to not let the enemy win (or perhaps in remembrance of a dead or separated sibling, someone they are fighting for or fighting to get back to)? Does someone paint over or destroy the graffitied symbol in some other scene, and does your protagonist react with grim silence, or kicking and screaming? Do others take up your protagonist's cause, so that in your climactic scene, that same symbol is graffitied on the walls of every building for ten blocks?

Identify the threshold action and then 5 times it can be repeated in ways that—if you write those 5 moments down on one piece of paper—will tell the story in miniature. Use that action to illustrate 5 crucial points in the story's central conflict, 5 points on the character's journey to who they eventually become at the end of your story.

The possibilities are endless and exciting. The key is to identify your threshold text and how it sets up questions and expectations for your story, so that you can hook the reader immediately, at the outset, with a specific sense of why this story matters, and so that you can work with that threshold in exciting ways later.

So: What threshold does your reader step over, to get into the story? And in what ways can your threshold text clue them into what matters in your story, and why? What rune is written on the door?

SOLVING THE SAGGY MIDDLE

We just talked about beginnings. Getting a firm handle on the thematic concerns of your story—and knowing exactly what thematic imagery you are *threading* through your narrative—also makes it easier to solve the plotting problem of the "saggy middle." That's the problem where, even if your beginning and your ending are crisp, clear, and compelling, the middle of the book bogs down. The pacing slows, the central conflicts of your story get mired in subplots or repetitive dialogue, and the story (and the reader) loses its excitement. Many storytellers fix the saggy middle by writing in a scene of high drama, high action, high stakes midway through the book—something that gets the blood pumping and refocuses the reader's attention on *why* the story and the happenings in it are important. In J.R.R. Tolkien's *The Fellowship of the Ring,* that's the dramatic horseback ride to the ford (as well as Gandalf's battle with the Balrog; we get it twice). In Lois McMaster Bujold's *A Civil Campaign*, it's the dinner banquet scene at which Miles Vorkosigan is attempting to impress and win over the object of his affections and every subplot in the story abruptly explodes messily at the table and all secrets come out at the worst (and most comedic) possible moment. In the movie *Braveheart*, it's the big battle in the middle when William Wallace suffers a terrible defeat and then learns that his closest ally has betrayed him.

In fact, in the old days, Hollywood always planned for a Big Thing to happen in the middle of the story, because, taking their cue from the world of live theatre and the Broadway musical, the filmmakers planned for an intermission in the middle of a long story—and to ensure that moviegoers returned after their bathroom break, you needed something really high stakes to happen right before the curtain dropped.

When you are alert to the thematic issues your story and its characters are wrestling with, then building the big dinner banquet or the car chase or the sudden reveal into the middle of your tale is much more than just a mechanical jolting of your plot into full throttle or into a crashing halt; it becomes an opportunity to invite your reader to *care* so much more about your story, at precisely the moment when, in a badly told tale with a saggy middle, there is the most risk that the reader will stop caring. This is the moment when you get to make the story matter twice as much to the reader. To do this, you do (at least) two things:

1. Write into the middle a very high-stakes choice for your protagonist. This may be a *wrong* choice that propels us into disastrous consequences, or it may be a *right* choice that nevertheless carries a terrible cost or requires a significant sacrifice.

2. Thread your thematic image and keyword into that choice—like the magic ingredient you add the

cauldron to give your brew its spice and its flavor—and add a new layer of meaning to that thematic image.

In Jim Butcher's urban fantasy novel *Changes*, the young wizard Harry Dresden suffers a debilitating injury during a battle with vampires in the middle of the book; in the dark, quiet scene when he lies in a bed afterward, he makes a terrible choice, bartering his soul and his allegiance to a supernatural being in return for the healing of his body that will permit him to return to battle and complete the rescue of someone he loves. All the thematic issues of the previous eleven and a half novels in his story bear down on that moment in that darkened room with formidable pressure. Dresden is driven by the desire to protect a child—as he, an orphan, had not been. That desire is at play. So, too, is his aloneness, his essential solitude, the orphan's conviction that no one can ultimately be trusted to be there for him. No one is coming to his rescue or his aid; it is *all on him.* And so, in that room, he hears a whisper in his ear—*you are alone*—and he makes his choice. The reader who has been following his tale feels that choice keenly and knows what it costs him. For Dresden, *alone* has always been the thematic keyword. If *adventure* is the rune written on Bilbo Baggins' door by others, *alone* was the rune written on Harry Dresden's. He has received the curse, *you will die alone*, and that has been his greatest fear; now, in this scene halfway through *Changes*, that fear is succeeded by the fear that someone he loves will die alone, if he is unable to rush to their rescue. In that scene at the darkened bed, the central thematic threads of the book vibrate with intensity in that moment, foregrounding for the reader the questions that matter: Are we ultimately alone? Do we each die alone? In our aloneness, what is our responsibility to others? How far can a man go to protect those he loves, without losing himself? What choice would *you* make, dear reader?

The stakes—the thematic stakes and the emotional stakes for the character—are written so clearly, and so the reader suddenly cares *very much* about this story. They have to read on. They have to find out whether Dresden's bargain will prove worth it, and what that bargain will ultimately mean, and whether, even if he loses himself, he will save his loved one.

That's how you fix the saggy middle. And it needn't be action—it could be a scene of dialogue in which your character suddenly learns something that turns their world inside out, and the choice they make in that moment—a choice of what to *feel,* maybe a choice of what to *do* or *say*—rewrites the course of the plot and rewrites part of the psychology of the character.

Exercise 29

Take a look at your manuscript, your outline, or just turn the idea for your story around and around in your head, and think about its middle. Come up with the ideas for three different options for a scene that could occur in the middle of the story. Regardless of the genre or the conventions that you either admire or defy as a writer:

- One is an action scene.
- One is a tense dialogue.

- One is an 'encounter' scene—in which the protagonist encounters an object, creature, or environment.

In each case, the character realizes something of thematic importance to the story and makes a choice. Perhaps the action scene involves choosing a side. Perhaps the dialogue scene reveals an infidelity at the worst possible moment. Perhaps the object encountered is a memento of the past that, once encountered, changes how the character and the reader feel about the present—or reminds them of what's *really* important. Once you have all three ideas jotted down on a piece of paper or in your document, consider the merits of each. Which scene appeals to you most, and why? Which would be most challenging to you to write? Which would prove most rewarding, if you pulled it off? And what steps would you take as a writer, in each case, to make the scene utterly riveting?

Exercise 30

Take a good look at the scene you chose in Exercise 29 as the scene most worthy of your effort. Now look at your thematic outline—the tool we discussed in Chapter 5. This outline records all the instances of your thematic keyword, the critical image that is threaded through your story. How can you either insert new instances or revisit and revise the existing ones to build toward the high-stakes scene that you're using to solve the saggy middle? What clues can you drop earlier that will pay off for the reader when that image recurs in the critical middle scene? Come up with three cases in which, in the earlier parts of your story, you can add clarity and detail to the thematic image or keyword so that when it appears in the middle scene, it acquires new layers of meaning that it didn't have before?

151

That last bit is the key. The *emotional* payoff of the middle scene is possible because the thematic question acquires a dimension and layer that it never had before. The question, *do we ultimately each live and die alone?* is the same question both before and after Harry Dresden's crucial choice, but the question acquires a different urgency and pathos during that scene in the dark quiet room, when his body lies broken and he faces the horrible fear that his *child* is living alone and will die alone, without his help. The theme means something more than it did in the preceding scenes. And so Harry—and the reader—care about it more intensely.

So, as a writer, in constructing or revising that high-stakes middle scene, you're addressing these questions:

1. What has my character just realized?
2. What choice is my character making?
3. What is the cost of *not* making the choice? What would be lost?
4. What is the cost of making it? What is lost?
5. How difficult can I make that choice for my character? How urgent? How do I make this feel like a *do-or-die* moment to them and to the reader?
6. What layer of meaning am I adding to the thematic question in this scene?
7. How will the consequences of this choice propel the character and the reader toward the closing scenes of the story?

Remember: Theme isn't separate from plot; it's what charges your plot with emotion and energy. Your thematic outline is what guides you in shaping and heightening your plot. *Plot* isn't a matter of adding car chases or shoot-em-ups or disastrously comedic dinner banquets simply for their own sake; plot isn't just spectacle. Plot is how you *tease* the reader (or torment them) with the story's thematic questions, it's how you hold up a question that matters and turn it around and around like a jewel, letting the reader see all its facets. And it's how you make the question and its answer *matter*, by making the reader and the character both strive and struggle for that answer. The answers that matter to us are answers we've *earned*, in toil and sweat, that we've paid the cost for, that we've lost something in order to attain. The way you get an exciting plot is by finding out: *How do I make it hard for the character—and the reader—to get this question answered? What are the most exciting and surprising ways to test that answer? Can I send them on a wild goose chase on the way? What does my character have to suffer or give up in order to get their question answered? What does my reader need to feel in order for that answer to mean something to them, as it does to me?* If your story includes a romance and the question is, *does true love conquer all?*, then what, precisely, will true love have to conquer, how hard will it be to conquer, and what will be attractive to your character about stepping away from the work of that conquest? What will make them pursue it? What setback in the middle of the story will paint that question in the starkest terms? That's what plot is for. When you know *why* your story matters, then you can write a plot that burns like torchfire in the heart. And you can heighten the intensity, the suspense, the momentum of that plot by thinking about just how much work it will be to get the answer to the question and to test it and to *believe* it, and by writing that work, that testing, into the story. Plot is how you test your characters, and it is how *they* test the answers they're getting to the question that matters most to them—the question that matters most to you.

By the way, there are many variations on this strategy of offering a mid-story climactic episode in which the story's themes are thrown into stark relief and the character's conflicts come temporarily to a point of collision. One of the most popular variations in Western storytelling for the past century or two has been the three-act structure, in which a story builds through three successive sequences of scenes or chapters. Each sequence mirrors and repeats the others, each time with variation, each time with more tension and higher stakes than the previous (until you reach the story's ultimate climax). Each of the three acts ends in a climax, and the three climaxes occur in the same location, or with the same characters, or with repeated lines of dialogue, or with some other shared element or circumstance that allows the second and third climaxes to each to build on the emotional fallout from the previous ones. Each delivers more tension than the previous. In *Arcane*, for example, we see three sequences of three episodes each, and each of these three 'acts' closes with a heartrending, climactic reunion between the sisters Vi and Jinx. Similarly, trilogies often adopt this three-act structure for use in a longer-form narrative. Each volume of *The Lord of the Rings* closes with a battle followed by a scene in which Frodo is separated from his companions—first at the breaking of the Fellowship, then when Sam believes him dead and goes on alone toward Mordor, and finally when Frodo and Sam part at the Grey Havens and Frodo takes ship across the sea. Each parting anticipates the next and comments on the previous, and the theme of fellowship is woven throughout each, and each asks questions about sacrifice, trauma, and the relationship between 'fellowship' and 'grief,' especially in the context of shared suffering and the sharing of each other's burdens. (The One Ring becomes, in these scenes, the example of the ultimate burden, heavy with responsibility, pain, and violent history.) Each parting scene asks to what extent it is in fact possible to share each other's burdens, and whether some burdens cannot be shared.

Exercise 31

You might not be using a three-act structure story, but imagine for a moment that you were. Imagine three scenes—three climaxes that would occur over the course of your story. Knowing what is thematically important to you and knowing the conflicts of your characters:

What location would you choose for these scenes?

What line of dialogue would be repeated, and how would the stakes be higher each time that exchange happens? Does the same character say that line each time, but with new layers of emotion and meaning, or do different characters say it in each scene that closes an act, so that the difference in emotional impact and thematic significance is achieved by the variation in who says it?

How would your characters be different in each of the three scenes? What would they have lived through between these scenes? This can help you map out the most exciting plot, because your plot is how your characters will live through what must be lived through before they meet again, or before that next version of the high-stakes conversation or high-stakes choice occurs.

In designing your plot, you can also play with not only how the climactic scenes in each act mirror and respond to each other, but how the opening scenes in each act do. Each act will have a threshold text that mirrors the previous one(s) and again highlights and complicates the thematic concerns in the story. You can also play with how the relationships and events in each act mirror and invert each other. For example, maybe Act 1 features two sisters who are then parted, and Act 2 features two lovers, and the story gets a lot of emotional and thematic mileage out of comparing and contrasting the two pairs. Perhaps each pair of women tackle the same thematic question together, but each pair does it a little differently. Then, as happened in *Arcane*, Act 3 can bring all three women together in the final climactic scene, driving the tension up as high as it can possibly go as we try to get a final answer to the question that burns like a sun at the heart of your story.

THE ART OF THE DENOUEMENT

Short story writer James Van Pelt suggests that "endings tell the reader what was important in the story. This is why endings can be hard to get right." The denouement helps the reader determine how to feel about the story and how to interpret what mattered about it, as the reader witnesses and reacts to how the *characters* feel about their actions and choices, and about the outcomes of those choices. The scene that follows the climax of your tale—or, depending on how you've structured your story, the epilogue, the coda, the closing flashback, or the cliffhanger—offers you rich opportunities to toss your thematic question back into the reader's hand, like a shiny, luscious fruit for them to bite into. Those closing moments comment on the plot, giving it its meaning or else providing the reader with the final riddle *they* need to answer.

One of my favorite examples is the epilogue to Lois McMaster Bujold's *Shards of Honor*. Throughout the novel, the reader has confronted the costs of honor and the question of *What is worth giving up your honor—and your allegiances—for?* Both of the novel's two primary characters have wrestled with this question and have faced terrible choices in striving to answer it. They have also had to answer, for themselves, each of them—singly and together—a second question, *How do you go on when your honor—your sense of yourself, your integrity, all that you had believed in and fought for—lies in shards at your feet?* Those two thematic questions give the novel its intensity, its pain, its momentum and drive.

Interestingly, the denouement—the epilogue scene— isn't told from either of the main characters' points of view, but through the perspective of medics cleaning up the space battlefield that the main characters have left in their wake. The medics sift the debris of dead and burnt-out battleships for bodies, for broken lives that need to be resolved and laid to rest. The scene is poignant and profound; one of the characters cleans a corpse and glances through his pockets for clues about who he was and what he was like while he still breathed, saying,

> Think of all the work he represents on somebody's part. Nine months of pregnancy, childbirth, two years of diapering, and that's just the beginning. Tens of thousands of meals, thousands of bedtime stories, years of school. Dozens of teachers. And all that military training, too. A lot of people went into making him.

What is worth giving up one's honor for? Life. Saving lives. Sometimes, the cost of honor is just too high, when paid in blood.

The medic is searching for the body of her daughter, and when she finds her at last, when she quietly cleans her daughter's body, dresses her in her uniform, and kisses her goodbye, she tells her coworker gently:

> Don't be afraid. The dead cannot hurt you. They give you no pain, except that of seeing your own death in their faces. And one can face that, I find.

Again, the scene touches on the fragility and high cost of life. And the closing line of the book is the coworker's reflection:

> Yes, he thought, the good face pain. But the great— they embrace it.

While not strictly an answer to the thematic questions (some questions are, in the end, more important to *ask* that to *answer*), that last line in the book does comment on the second of the two thematic questions, that of how to go on when your honor lies in shards at your feet. You have to "embrace" the pain of shattered honor and the pain of loss and the pain of grief, because that which you still have, that which you *haven't* lost—life (your own, and the lives you've saved)—is infinitely precious. A lot of work went into making you, and a lot of work went into each life that has been saved. That is precious.

Bujold's beautiful denouement emphasizes all of this—providing commentary on the story and why this story matters and how this story might go on mattering to us once we turn the last page and close the book—both by showing and telling. Bujold *shows* us by having the last scene in the tale told through the eyes of medics searching a battlefield for the dead, because each life is worth honoring in that way. And she *tells* us too, by commenting explicitly on the themes of the book through the mouths of her characters in that scene. And if one of the characters serves the reader as a 'sage,' a mature older voice dispensing nuggets of wisdom, that sagecraft is earned because it was purchased with pain; the medic is a mother who put all that work into her daughter, and now must tend to and honor her body. Who better to speak to us, at the end of this story, about the value of life and the high cost of honor?

Finally, the thematic keyword and image that are first given to us in the book's title, *Shards of Honor*, are present and central throughout the scene—*honor*, in the shape of the dead soldiers' uniforms and the medic's ritual of cleaning and preparing them for their final rest, and *shards* of honor because the honored soldiers are dead, their bodies broken.

But maybe *shards* can be beautiful too. And maybe loss can be embraced, even as the bereaved mother embraces her dead child after dressing her one last time in her uniform.

That is a scene that I will never forget, and it is one of the scenes that made that story one I will never forget.

In your own story, in your own final scene, how might you snap your thematic questions into that kind of crystal clarity?

Exercise 32

Here's an experiment. Write two versions of your story's final scene:

1. In one version, have the scene told from the perspective of your main character, and have the answer to the thematic question or the commentary on it spoken in their voice, thought in their head, demonstrated by their action, or otherwise presented to the reader through their eyes.

2. In a second version, try the Bujold method and write an epilogue in which the commentary is presented through the perspective of a minor character or even a late addition to the cast. Make sure it is earned, though—even in that brief epilogue scene, there must be stakes. The actions and words in that scene need to matter not only as commentary on the larger story but in their own context; they need to matter within this one scene. Just as with Bujold's medic searching for the body of her child on a battlefield, there must be a cost

for your viewpoint character, so that their commentary is purchased at a price and does not come cheaply to the reader.

Having done this, consider:

- Which scene is more compelling to you? Why?
- Are there elements in the *less* compelling scene that you want to preserve and use? If so, what are some ways in which you can import those elements into the other scene?

That is a beautiful thing about writing—when a scene doesn't work, you can still cannibalize its better parts for use elsewhere.

Here is an example of a denouement that is all showing and no telling—the final page of *The Lord of the Rings*. Evil has been defeated (for the time being) and Frodo Baggins has departed across the sea, and his companion Samwise Gamgee returns home, embraces his wife and children, and pauses at the door of Bag End, which is now his home. "Well," he says, "I'm back." It's a simple ending, befitting a simple character and the love of simple things—family and gardening and friendship and good cheer—that has permeated this tale of wizards and kings and epic happenings. In the first pages of this toolkit, I mentioned one of the thematic statements in *The Lord of the Rings*—that all we have to do is decide what to do with the time that is given to us. We have learned over the course of the story that this decision is informed by our past, by the examples (good and bad) of those who have gone before us, and so Sam's life will always be informed and deepened by the memory of his time with Frodo, and of all that they fought and suffered and achieved. But in the end, what matters most—what is truly worth the final page of a thousand-page story—is the simple act of returning home to one's family after the struggle. Of focusing on the present, of the time that is given to us, more than on the past or the future. "Well, I'm back"—with all the bittersweetness and the simple pleasure and the quiet joy of that phrase—is the final one-liner of the book. None of this had to be *told* to us; as readers, we feel it. That ending feels poignant and quiet and *right*. The story earned that ending for us. The ending in my example of *The Grandmother's Quilt* in Chapter 4 is that kind of ending, too—quiet but immensely meaningful. Just two women working on a quilt, putting a family or a relationship back together as they stitch together those colored squares.

Exercise 33

In the previous exercise, I asked you to write commentary on your story's thematic questions into the final scene. This time, imagine a scene that needs no commentary, a scene whose final image, act, or location does the work for us. What final image or phrase could you end your story with?

CLOSING REMARKS

Speaking of endings, we have come now to the ending of this book, though in fact this end is only the beginning of the next chapter in the adventure *you* have embarked upon, an adventure in which you can put some of what you have learned in this book—whatever struck you as most useful—to work as you craft your own fiction. I hope the suggestions and exercises in this book have helped you sharpen your focus and define the thematic questions that will energize your characters and ignite your plot. When I think about what you will create, I get excited.

You can do this. Inside you are stories that *matter*; all that's needed is the craft to tell them well and the courage to tell them with the thematic intensity and velocity your stories deserve. Let yourself be relentless in seeking out what matters in your stories, and let yourself be playful in surfacing those matters for the reader. While it is true that life is brief and that there is only so much time to read and so much time to listen, I truly believe that humanity is not complete until everyone's story has been heard and can be heard—and that if we could hear everyone's tale told truly and well (if we could look, as Rasha yearns to in *Ansible*, at the mosaic of all humanity), every tale would wow us. Tell yours and make it the very best you can. Trust that we'll be wowed! Yours is a good story.

STANT LITORE
JANUARY 2022

AFTERWORD | THE RISKS OF UNEXAMINED QUESTIONS

BY THE TIME YOU'VE REACHED THIS PAGE, you've finished this book, checked out all the exercises, and you are probably ready to put pen to paper or fingertips to keyboard and make something *amazing*. This afterword doesn't share additional techniques, just precautions. Words of advice. Warning of blunders. It's about what could happen if you are not intentional about crafting the themes of your fictional work. Don't let these final pages daunt you, but let them encourage you to hone your awareness of what you are doing with your story, and why.

Let's talk briefly about unforeseen implications and unintended consequences. As soon as a reader picks up on a thematic question raised by your story—whether they are doing so consciously or not—the story begins to *matter* to them, whether they accept it and revel in it; wrestle with it; or reject it. And as soon as your story starts to *matter*, this entertainment you've designed and delivered to the reader acquires higher stakes. Whether slightly or significantly higher depends on the story and the nature of the thematic inquiry. This is where it becomes possible to blunder if you're unaware of the questions your story is raising.

What do I mean by that? Let's take a popular novel, *Me Before You* by Jojo Moyes, which was a bestseller and also got a movie deal. Financially, the book was very much a success, and it certainly has many fans. The novel is also hated by many readers with disabilities and their families. This is because the novel raises thematic implications that the author doesn't appear to have considered; these implications may remain invisible to some readers who are not disabled themselves, but these implications are glaringly visible to disabled readers and their loved ones. The novel is a love story, and at the end, the male love interest commits suicide to (lovingly) remove himself from the protagonist's life so that she will not be burdened and held back by him and so that her own life can flourish.

Do you see what happened there? The premise raises a thematic question, *Are disabled people a burden? Would it be better for able people if disabled people weren't here?* And the novel answers, *Yes*, pretty definitively. This doesn't present a problem for some able readers because either (a) they may not pick up on the thematic question, as other questions about the nature of love and relationships are presented to them as primary, or (b) some may implicitly agree with the *Yes* answer without consciously thinking about it, and the story doesn't ever call on them to examine or question that implicit agreement; the narrative appears unaware of the question it has raised. Disabled readers know that the thematic question—and the answer given before the end of the novel—has toxic and damaging implications. This isn't because of any malice on the author's part; it's because the author neglected to take a good look at what thematic questions were being raised by the premise of the story. Once those questions are visible to the reader, an author doesn't have the luxury of not noticing them, because readers expect that the story will address them.

A student of mine was writing a novel in which an introverted and unhappy, neurodivergent woman ends up stranded inside the body of her counterpart in an alternate reality; the author's original plan for the novel was that the woman's double would be an extroverted fashion designer, at ease with social situations and relationships—and also neurotypical. Do you see the thematic implications being raised? There's an implicit equation that *neurodivergent* equals socially inept, sad, and lonely, and that the fix is to somehow become (or act) *neurotypical*—to fit in. That is a theme that might prove unsettling or abusive to many neurodivergent readers. The author, to their credit, recognized the problem at once when it was raised, and decided to make both characters neurodivergent, thus removing the damaging implication while still fulfilling their intent of exploring neurodivergent characters. I look forward to the finished novel; it may prove an exciting and moving story.

It is not an uncommon thing for a writer (and, sometimes, their editor) to remain unaware of the darker implications of their story's premise—or to simply not care. The author of *Save the Pearls* appears to have been unaware of the thematic implications and racial stereotypes suggested by a narrative in which a young white woman flees through a post-apocalyptic world while terrified of pursuit and capture by violent dark-skinned rapists. The script for the film *Passengers* never adequately addresses the ethical issue and thematic implications of taking a story about a man in isolation who abducts a woman from her life and family so that she must be his companion, and then telling that as a love story. Many other examples might occur to us, both from fiction that failed to achieve much note and from commercially successful fiction, too.

The point isn't that you need to write a story that upsets no one; only (some) beach reads achieve that. That is rarely the goal; I would say the goal is to make your readers *feel* deeply—whether you're out to make them cry, make them laugh, make them wonder and delight, or make them angry. You want the reader to feel as deeply about your story as *you* and your characters do. That's why we're talking about theme, after all; theme is why stories matter to us even after we've finished reading them. The stories we remember speak something that we feel is real and true, or shake us up by questioning something that we used to believe was real and true. So, good stories will often upset people. But you want to upset people because of things you did *on purpose*, fully aware of your authorial choices and their implications—not because of things you did *on accident*, while unaware of what you were doing.

It's critical that you don't leave your thematic questions unexamined (by you). Especial care might be advisable when you are telling a story that includes characters who are very different from you—especially if those characters look similar to people who are marginalized in our society. In those cases, it's both prudent and responsible to do the research, which means being willing to ask the questions.

Conferring with writer colleagues or readers who are of diverse demographics can help. There are also *Writing the Other* webinars and virtual workshops offered by K. Tempest Bradford, Nisi Shawl, and other noted writers at www.writingtheother.com; these are fantastic resources for writers. When you have a completed manuscript, one option is also to hire a sensitivity reader to spot potential issues with representation in the story.

There are other ways for a story to fail to deliver on its thematic promises, and many of these have nothing to do with questions of race, gender, ableism, or privilege. Sometimes, a story can raise thematic questions that are simply left unanswered or badly answered by the story; in such cases, your story may not cause the reader hurt or anger, but it might leave them deeply unsatisfied—by accident.

For example, suppose you create a science fiction story about a woman and a robot who fall in love. The premise itself raises questions like *What is love? Who can experience it? Can a machine feel?* Or maybe, *What is the definition of being human? (Can a robot be human?)* The question is raised inevitably by the premise of a robot who loves a human being, and the story could offer some very elegant treatments of that question. For example, the story could propose answers such as *Anyone capable of loving is human,* or *We become fully human when we learn to love.* The story could also leave the question unanswered and keep the reader on their toes by offering a play of mind, proposing first one possibility and then another, without ever conclusively telling us which one is real. Maybe the narrative does this by raising the question in our minds of whether the robot can love, and, as the story unfolds, at some moments we think that yes, the robot can—but at other moments in the story, both we and the story's female protagonist are uncertain. Maybe, the author wants us a bit uneasy. Maybe this isn't a romance story; maybe it's a thought experiment and we readers are guinea pigs.

Those are all examples of how you could handle the themes implicit in such a tale. But what will leave readers unfulfilled and likely to forget the story (or even fail to finish it) is if the author does none of these things— neither offering answers nor a play of mind nor examining that thematic question of identity (and of how and whether our human identity and our capacity for love are connected). If the story simply raises or implies the question and then *drops* it, that can be incredibly frustrating to a reader. It's a way of inviting the reader to a banquet and then neither seating them at the banquet nor closing the door in their face but simply wandering around your house having forgotten that you were offering a banquet at all. Readers want to feel that they're in good hands, that the storyteller knows what they're doing. And if their expectations are going to be frustrated, it should be clear what purpose that frustration or misdirection serves.

The best way to avoid this is to take an evening and sit down with your story—maybe with a friend or writer colleague present to serve as an interlocutor and fellow researcher—and ask chains of questions:

- What is the central premise of my plot?
- How will that premise be understood by readers of backgrounds other than my own?

- What thematic questions are implied by this premise?
- Does my story address those questions or drop them?
- Does my story propose answers to those questions?
- How will those answers be understood by readers of backgrounds other than my own?
- Do I have a specific 'message' I think my tale is conveying?
- If so, does the story *earn* that message and demonstrate it effectively?
- Are there aspects of my story and its characters or its world that implicitly challenge, contradict, or shed doubt on the validity or reliability of that message?

A final caution about 'messages': No writer is more likely to prove oblivious to the implications of their story than the writer who sets out at the beginning to build a story explicitly for the purpose of conveying a specific 'message.' Stories are not the same as sermons, though sermons can include stories and stories, sermons. The message arises out of the story; the story doesn't arise out of the message. If you set out to tell a message in the form of a story, it is very hard to make that *feel* true. That is what preaching or teaching is for; storytelling engages the heart first, then the head. Whatever 'message' or whatever beliefs burn in your own heart, whatever drives you most deeply—those are the messages that will come out naturally in your story. It's not something you manufacture. Your job as a writer is to be alert to what is already coming out in your story, so that you can help it grow—and shape the most gripping story you can.

As writers, we play *and* we put in the work. Make your story unforgettable by being intentional about its themes, and by ensuring your narrative *earns* those themes. Make each scene and each character in the book count. Make us want to quote *your* Gandalf or your Sam Gamgee or your protagonist the next time we—or our loved ones—are in trouble, the next time we're walking and whistling in the dark, the next time *we* have a choice to make, the next time we need someone's words or their example to make sense of what we're feeling or going through in our own lives.

And, if you can, give that experience to readers of different backgrounds and social positions. Let many of us be moved by your story. Craft that story so that it matters to us, too. Make it a story we can't stop reading, that we can't stop thinking about and talking about. Go and do *that*. Good luck. Go write.

ABOUT THE AUTHOR

STANT LITORE writes about zombies, aliens, and tyrannosaurs. He does not currently own a starship or a time machine but would rather like to. He lives in Aurora, Colorado with his three children and hides from visitors in the basement library beneath a heap of toy dinosaurs, tattered novels, comic books, incomprehensibly scribbled drafts, and antique tomes. He has taught for Clarion West, Writing the Other, Apex Writers, and Pikes Peak Writers. He is working on his next novel, or several. You can read some of his current fiction by looking up *Ansible, The Running of the Tyrannosaurs, The Zombie Bible,* or *Dante's Heart.* However, doing so may have unpredictable effects, and Stant offers no assurances that you will emerge from any of these stories unscathed. Best leave all non-essentials behind, take with you only what you need to survive, and venture into the books cautiously and ready to call for backup. Enjoy, and good luck.

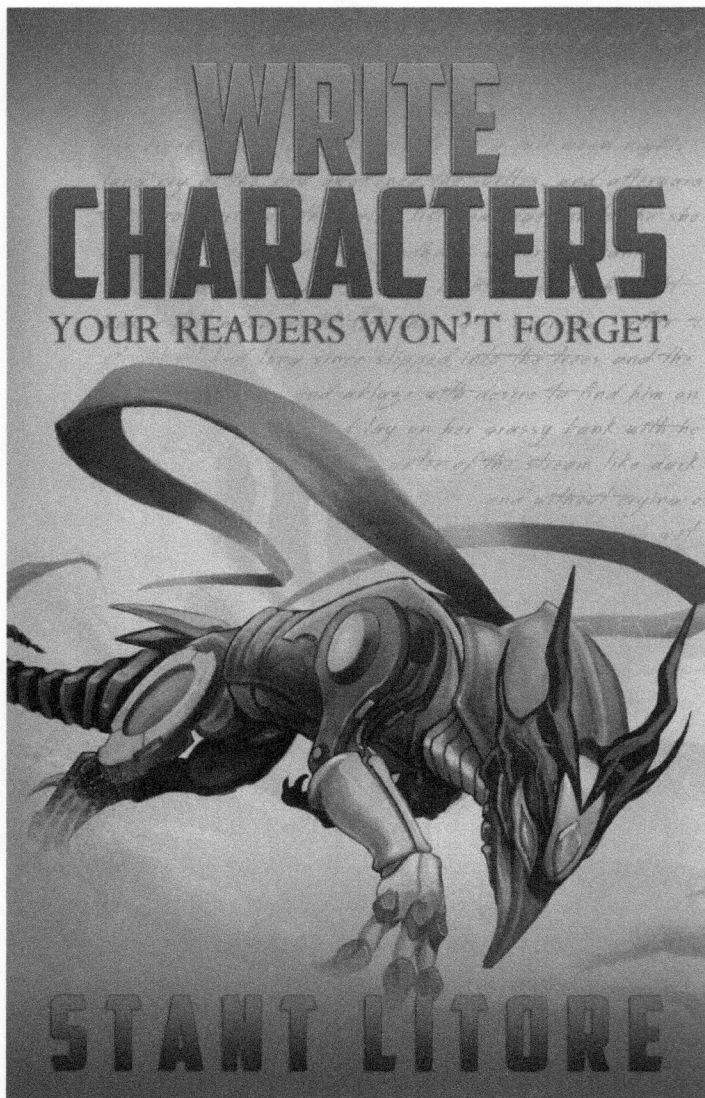

*If you enjoyed this book,
I hope you will also try:*

WRITE CHARACTERS
YOUR READERS WON'T FORGET

"I just don't care enough about your character."

Write Characters Your Readers Won't Forget is a toolkit for addressing that issue. Packed with 30 exercises, abundant examples, and practical strategies, this guidebook will help you write unforgettable characters who "come alive" on the page, create compelling dialogue, and chart more breathtaking emotional journeys for your characters.

ISBN 978-1942458050

AVAILABLE AT:

BOOKSHOP.ORG

AMAZON

BARNES & NOBLE ONLINE

STANTLITORE.COM
(direct from the author)

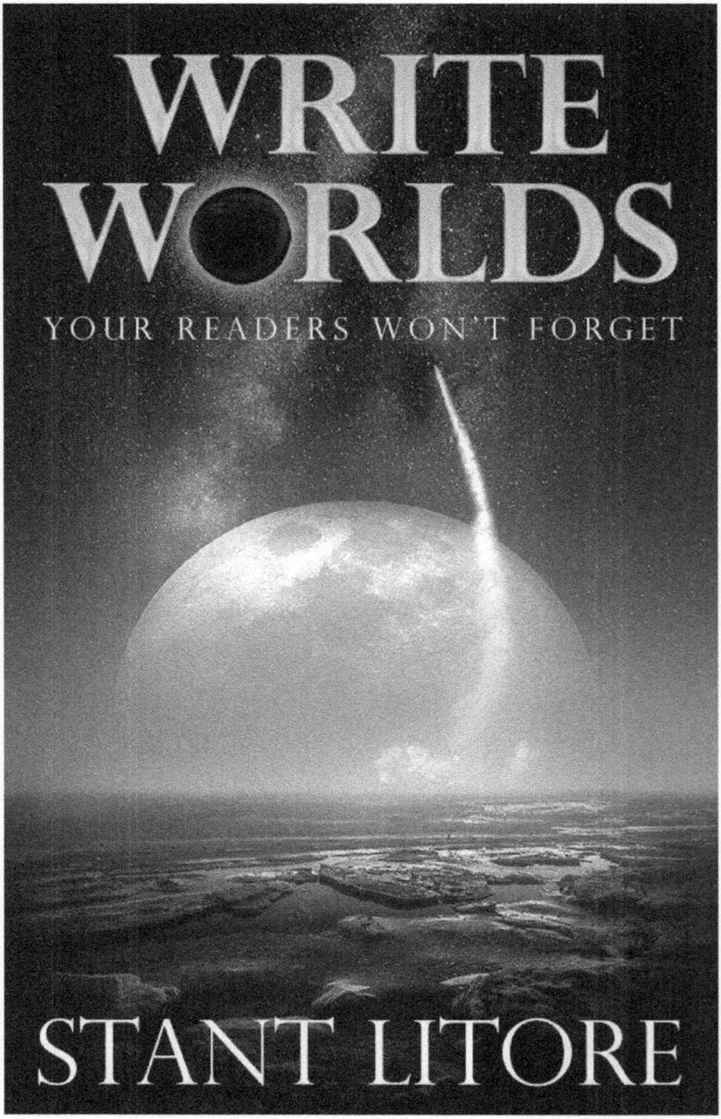
WRITE
WORLDS
YOUR READERS WON'T FORGET
STANT LITORE

WRITE WORLDS
YOUR READERS WON'T FORGET

"There are other worldbuilding books out there; this is the one you want." - Travis Heerman, author of the *Ronin* trilogy and *Death Wind*.

Like a god, you get to invent a world. Maybe several. But how do you make these worlds that readers want to visit? How do you make them worlds that readers never want to leave? In *Write Worlds Your Readers Won't Forget*, explore how to create unforgettable environments, creatures, and cultures in 33 intensive exercises.

ISBN 978-1942458302

AVAILABLE AT:

BOOKSHOP.ORG

AMAZON

BARNES & NOBLE ONLINE

STANTLITORE.COM
(direct from the author)

www.ingramcontent.com/pod-product-compliance
Lightning Source LLC
Chambersburg PA
CBHW030830090426
42737CB00009B/944